The Legacy

THE LEGACY OF THE BLUES
Samuel Charters

A glimpse into the art and the lives
of twelve great bluesmen
An informal study

DA CAPO PRESS

Library of Congress Cataloging in Publication Data

Charters, Samuel Barclay.
  The legacy of the blues.

  (A Da Capo paperback)
  Reprint of the ed. published by Calder &
Boyers, London.
  Bibliography: p.
  Discography: p.
  1. Blues (Songs, etc.) — United States — History
and criticism. 2. Afro-American musicians —
Biography. I. Title.
ML3556.C475L4 1977 784 76-51399
ISBN 0-306-80054-3

ISBN: 0-306-80054-3

First Paperback Printing 1977

The Legacy of the Blues by Samuel Charters first published in
1975 in London by Calder & Boyars Ltd.

First American Edition, 1977, by Da Capo Press, Inc.

Photo credits: Ann Charters; pp. x, 20 (J. D. Short), 92; Hans
Ekestang; pp. 20 (Big Joe Williams), 48, 122; D. Redfern; p. 34;
Karl-Erik Hägglund; p. 60; Samuel Charters; pp. 74, 172; Hans
Lychou; p. 110; Lasse Lindedal; p. 132; Jan Ytterberg; p. 156
(Memphis Slim and Eddie Boyd); Jim Taylor; p. 144. Grateful
acknowledgement is made to *Jefferson*, the Swedish blues maga-
zine, for permission to print photographs from their archives.

Published by Da Capo Press,

10 9 8 7 6 5 4

A member of the Perseus Book Group
All Rights Reserved

Manufactured in the United States of America

For
Dag and Viveca

CONTENTS

Leg-a-cy (Middle English *legacie*, from Middle French or Medieval Latin; Middle French *legacie*, from Medieval Latin *legatia* — office or jurisdiction of a legate, from Latin *legatus* — past participle of *legare*, to send as a deputy, bequeath) . . .

3a. Something received (as from an ancestor or predecessor) resembling or suggestive of a gift by will. b. something coming from the past (as from an age, a time, or an action)

ANOTHER AMERICA

Southside Chicago

ANOTHER AMERICA

It is clear that the black man and the black woman live a separate life in the United States — that there is what has been called 'another America'. But how is it defined? How is it different? Certainly it's different because it's black, but what is the nature of the blackness? Is it more than just the color of the skin? Is it, as well, a culture and tradition? For years there has been a continuing debate on the question of the uniqueness of the black society in America. It is a question of what, if anything, survived the slave experience and left its mark on the society that developed first in the rural South, then in the ghetto slums. Is there some quality in this life that is more than just an adaptation of a completely acculturated black group — a poor minority — to the surrounding white society? Or is there something else there; some traces of a cultural background that's completely different from it?

Physically, it isn't difficult to recognize the other America. The sullen, heavy face of poverty looks out of the doors of the shabby tenements, it lurks deep at the end of the darkened hallways, in the shadows where the single, bare bulb doesn't reach. Because we have been forced to see — because the blues, among other things, has made it possible for us to see — we do know that the poverty's there, that the other America is a grim parody of the America in the advertisements. It is familiar, all of it, but it's easier to try to forget about it.

In 1970 the median family income in the United States for whites was $9,961; for blacks it was $6,067, more than a third less. The average income — not the median figure — was even lower, with the average black family earning only half as much as the white. In the jargon of the Census Bureau, as covered by the news services:

> Black family incomes were lower than white in 1970 for a number of reasons. One, the bureau makes clear, was that blacks were paid less than whites for comparable work. The median earnings of white male 'professional, managerial, and kindred workers' in 1970 was $11,108. The median for the same category of blacks was $7,659. Among 'craftsmen, foremen, and kindred workers,' the white median was $8,305, the black median, $5,921.

> Smaller but similar black-white discrepancies appeared even among male laborers and female clerks.

> A second reason also showed up in the numbers. A tenth of all U.S. families — 5.5 million out of 51.2 million — had women at their heads in 1970; but almost one-fourth of all black families — 1.33 million out of 4.8 million — had no male wage-earner at their heads at census time. The women heading one-third

of them worked. The other two-thirds did not.

The result was that this quarter of all black families had a median income of only $4,396 in 1970. The effect was to drag down appreciably the median for all black families.

The figures go on; the statistics go on. 41% of all black children are being raised below the income level considered the poverty line — in the city ghettos unemployment rates are 18%-25%, compared with a national average of 5%-6%. It goes on and on — the face of poverty just inside the broken doorways, outside the paint peeling window sills. Only a black can tell another black of what has to be endured on the psychic level when it's necessary to walk into a room filled with white faces. But the Census figures are something else. We can write them down — look at them, understand them on our own terms; even if we never do anything about them.

In a more immediate sense the other America is the world of Juke Boy Bonner in the Houston ghetto, it's the dark bayous close to Robert Pete Williams' house, it's Big Joe Williams' small southern town, the Chicago neighborhoods where Mighty Joe Young works with his little band. Black America is thirteen percent of all of America — twenty-three million people. In one way highly visible because of its centering in the major cities, but otherwise almost out of sight. As a world it's shabby, run-down, and crowded. It's angry and resentful. It's violent and unstable. At its lowest level it's drug ridden and alcoholic.

It's a world that has been photographed, described, analyzed, and discussed — since the explosion of the black ghettos in the 1960's there has been a corresponding explosion in the studies, articles, symposiums, and polemics. It has been, sadly, like the proliferation of studies about American education that followed the launching of the first earth satellite by the Soviet Union. The pretence has been stripped away that the black is a docile victim, and he has emerged as a strident claimant of his rights as a citizen. Predictably, the America that created the ghettos is now trying to understand how such a thing as the ghettos could exist.

But it is as unfair to describe all of the life that black men and woman live in the cities as this kind of unrelenting, drab struggle as it is to describe black life in the kind of happy Sambo terms that southern whites did. There is within the ghetto a wide range of personality and experience. There are within the ghettos even pockets of affluence, like Harlem's 'Sugar Hill'. It is a society with as much variety as the surrounding white society, and there is certainly within the group an established social stratification. There are thousands of black families who aren't part of the statistics of poverty and disease and crime, and to suggest that these are characteristic of the entire society is to look at the problem from a racist view. Certainly these are clearly problems related to poverty, and through systematic discrimination the black society has been kept poor. It is important to consider that the blues system of values is a poverty system, but that its closest identification is only with the lowest economic level of this black society.

The role of the bluesman, in itself, is a series of contradictions. The system of reference in the blues is to this poverty system — shabby rooms and hungry nights, bad liquor, broken home life and economic uncertainty. But often the singers themselves have done well — they have substantial incomes and a fair degree of personal stability. Certainly within the framework of their own society they would be considered successes. But what they sing is clearly involved with their audience, and the picture of poverty within their music doesn't alter. They are professional entertainers, as well as creative artists, and they do what the audience wants them to do.

The fact of this duality, and the persistence of the poverty system in the blues, is a strong indication of the depth of the involvement of the community with the mores and descriptions of the blues. At one level there is

14

a strong universality to the music, but at a more immediate level there is an oblique, but unmistakeable reflection of the 'otherness' of black America in its popular song, which for many years — as the community fought its way to a more open place in American society — was the blues.

It has always been difficult for many people to accept the reality of a unique black culture in the United States — since there were few generally agreed cultural features, and even those that were almost unmistakeable couldn't be adequately explained. Since Europe became obsessively rational and mechanistic in the eighteenth century the tendency has always been to dismiss anything that couldn't be explained. Much of the early confusion has stormed around the effort to find direct Africanisms in the life of the black American today. The most famous of these early efforts was the study by Melville Herskowitz, which related a wide range of characteristics — from posture to the use of handkerchiefs — to African models. Some of what he pointed out was valuable, some more controversial. There were many critical responses that insisted that what he saw as African was shared with the rest of the country's poor — and because the African elements were so indistinct the tendency has been to dismiss them.

But it is clear that there are strong differences between the two societies, white and black, despite years of living together in the same countryside, the same towns, the same city streets. It's a difference that can't be explained away by pointing to the lack of obvious Africanisms. To be African is to be tribal, and the de-tribalization of the slave society effectively removed the strongest sources of cultural identity. But there has been another source of what must be considered a distinct pattern of life and society — and this has been in the experience of the black man in the United States. The sociologist Robert Blauner has discussed some of the impact of this experience in an article 'Black Culture: Myth or Reality?':

15

There is a sociological plausibility to the argument that Negroes are only Americans with black skins. As Frazier stressed, the manner in which North American slavery developed — in contrast to Caribbean and South American slavery — eliminated the most central African traits, those elements of ethnicity which European and Asian immigrants brought to this country: language, dress, religions, and other traditional institutions, a conscious identification with an overseas homeland. Basic as is this critical difference, it misses the point in assuming that there is only one geometric process — that model of European ethnic assimilation — through which nationality, cultures and the dominant American ethos have interacted. What must be understood is the uniqueness of the Afro-American condition, an essential aspect of which has been a deviant cultural experience that to some degree is the reverse of those of the traditional ethnic minorities. . . .

. . . Central to my argument against the conventional position is the thesis that the *ghetto subculture involves both lower-class and ethnic characteristics.* Poverty is only one source of black culture, and, as I shall attempt to prove, even the lower-class traits and institutions in Negro life have been modified by strictly ethnic values. Among the other sources of black culture are Africa, slavery, the South, Emancipation and Northern migration, and above all, *racism.* In other words, one of the main sources for the shared culture of the black American is the shared experience of struggling to live in America. After three hundred years it isn't surprising that there should be an extensive and rich new culture. Since the white society has refused to allow the black man a role in their world the black American has developed his own, fused out of elements from a dim African past, but gathering into it some of the responses to the unique situation he has had to face.

The blues is a remarkably clear reflection of this

otherness — not only in its larger themes, but in its smaller details as well. It has long been clear that some of the major themes of the blues — lonely travel, family disorientation, poverty — even though they were all presented through the overwhelming blues obsession with the love relationship — mirrored the social disorientation of the other America. It is not only in the broad outlines, but as much in the myriad small nuances of phrase and attitude.

A line of Mighty Joe Young's,

Now, it's early in the morning,
the stores ain't open yet,
I need a little something, you all
to get my throat wet . . .

This image is immediately of an income group that doesn't have enough money to keep a supply of liquor in the house. It could be argued that there is nothing in this phrase specifically suggesting that, but it is in a blues context, and this context has been — as a system of reference — relentlessly descriptive of a poverty environment. Juke Boy Bonner's songs often specifically relate to the separateness of the black society:

My mother passed on when I was just about eight,
I started to learn I was growin' up in a world of hate . . .

But there is something just as specific in his imagery in a blues song like 'Tired Of The Greyhound Bus':

I'm gettin' tired ridin' that old Greyhound,
I'm gettin' tired ridin' that old Greyhound,
I ain't no worry 'bout the service,
but they just keep on layin' my bags around.
Well, I went to Chicago to pay my debts, went there to
play the gig,
Chicago, to pay my debts, and I went there to play my
gig.
When I got to the station,
I didn't have nothin' to play it with. . . .

Most performers don't have to sit up on cross country buses to make personal appearances — and most bluesmen don't either — but their audience does, and the Greyhound is a symbol that has done long service in the blues.

I don't mean to suggest by this that the blues is unique in the fact that it presents the real face of the society. The music of the poverty areas in the white society tends to mirror — to somewhat the same extent — the details of the poverty. When white country music talks about beer it's talking about a symbol of the social life. Middle class song more often would mention cocktails, and the distinction is social as well as economic. And it isn't enough to suggest that the blues simply mirrors those aspects of the black society that are inextricably bound up with its poverty. As the African leader Tom Mboya wrote,

I find here (in America) a complete misunderstanding of what African culture really means. An African walks barefoot or wears sandals made out of old tires not because it is his culture but because he lives in poverty. We live in mud and wattle huts and buy cheap Hong Kong fabrics not because it is part of our culture but because these are conditions imposed on us today by poverty and by limitations in technical, educational, and other resources. White people have often confused the symbols of our poverty with our culture. I would hope that black people would not make the same mistake.

To find in the blues only the symbols of poverty would be to miss the greatness of the blues legacy. It is more than these physical details that fill the blues. There is, as well, a sense of the great vitality of the black culture. It is a culture that has been forced down to the lowest economic levels of the American social scene, but that has still managed to fashion out of its meager materials a society with a richness and variety that is equalled by the ranging freedoms of its popular song, the blues. With the rise of the black middle class new musical forms and styles have emerged, but the root language for it all is still the blues and when finally black historians and black sociologists begin the assessment of what has been the cultural achievement of the years in America, it is to the blues that they will have to turn for many of their answers.

Big Joe Williams and J.D. Short

Big Joe Williams

J.D. Short

SOME VISIBLE MEN
- Big Joe Williams and J.D. Short

One of the realities of the black experience in America is that, as Ralph Ellison wrote, the black man and woman are 'invisible' to the white world that surrounds them. 'I am an invisible man ... I am invisible, understand, simply because people refuse to see me. Like the bodiless heads you see sometimes in circus sideshows, it is as though I have been surrounded by mirrors of hard distorting glass. When they approach me they see only my surroundings, themselves, or figments of their imagination — indeed, everything and anything except me. . .' It has always been the harsh truth that black Americans have been swept out of the way, pushed aside, and left to make what they could of whatever the white society didn't want. Even in towns or cities where black and white lived side by side — in the same neighborhoods, sometimes in the same buildings — the white didn't *see* his neighbor. He only saw the color of the skin, and the response between them stopped at that unyielding boundary.

But there were moments when people began to see a little — when they tried to rub their eyes free of the shadows their backgrounds had left over them — and for many young white Americans the first black man they ever *saw* was a blues singer. First it was the raw strength of the music that forced them to listen — then the voices — then the singers themselves. They were visible men — they had a size and a dimension, and one of these dimensions was the language of the blues itself. Whatever else the blues was it was a language; a rich, vital, expressive language that stripped away the misconception that the black society in the United States was simply a poor, discouraged version of the white. It was impossible not to hear the differences. No one could listen to the blues without realizing that there are two Americas. It was in the voice, it was in the words, it was in the obsessions of the blues. The rough, grimy poetry of the blues was the clouded mirror of the ghetto life the white American never saw — and it was, at the same time, the personal poetry of the men who sang it. For the first time their faces began to have an identity, their fingers and bodies began to have a substance. In the voice, for the first time, it was possible to see the man who was singing.

Of all these men, of all these voices, one of the most visible is Big Joe Williams — as his cousin J.D. Short was visible; two intensely visible men who stretched out, took up space, and held on to their own place in the world. For J.D. it was a narrower world — his room in the shabby St. Louis ghetto, the barrooms where he occasionally played. For Joe it has become all of the United States and most of Europe. When I would see them it was in St. Louis — when Joe had left Chicago, where he usually lived, and drifted back to St. Louis to play for a few dollars a night in one of the local dance halls. Sometimes they'd stay in a battered room together, but J.D. was usually with his wife, and Joe would get a room not far away in the same neighborhood. It was at a time when St. Louis was going through the first phases of 'urban renewal', which meant that square blocks of the ghetto had been leveled and the people who'd been living in the houses had been forced to get out of the area or crowd even more closely together in the buildings that were left.

It was a strange half-world in the ghetto ruins during those years. In some blocks buildings had been left standing — some were deserted, even though the windows were shuttered and the doors shut so they looked as if somebody might come back to them. Others were crumbling hulks — the windows torn out of their frames and the doors splintered in; the floors covered with glass and old newspapers, smelling of urine and wine and decay. But people were still living in some of them. At night, across the rubble, in the tall black shape of a lonely building, you'd see lights coming from windows, a dim bulb over the doorway. Most of the people still in them were old. They'd been living in the building for more years than they could remember and they couldn't bring themselves to get out, despite the pressure from the slum authorities. When Joe would ask me to meet him it was usually in a room in one of the old buildings. Either he'd rented the room for a few weeks, or he'd moved in with somebody he knew. Usually, on the hot summer nights when I'd find my way through the darkness, both Joe and J.D. would be waiting for me.

I think of them most often in short-sleeved shirts, pressed trousers a little threadbare — J.D. usually in a straw hat that he used to fan himself with. Since the

23

buildings were going to be torn down as soon as the people had gotten out of them there wasn't much maintenance. The hallways were swept, but any broken stairs were left as they were. The wallpaper was pulled down when it started to peel off the walls, so the hallways usually had bare white plaster spots as you walked down through the noise of people living behind the scarred doorways. Most of the floors inside the apartments had two or three different pieces of lino-leum that didn't match with each other — red and white stripes half covering a discolored pattern of mauve flowers, and that worn away to dim green marbling underneath it all. Most of the time there was a bed in the room where we sat to talk — a dresser crowded with medicine and photographs and souvenirs, two or three hard chairs. Neither Big Joe or his cousin were tall, and despite their bulk they weren't fat. They were strong, heavy men, their bodies formed by the labor they'd done before they were even adolescents. You couldn't help looking at them — you couldn't help responding to their presence in the bright glare of the room's dangling bulb.

It was true, as well, that sometimes the physical presence was all you could respond to. Joe is often almost impossible to understand when he's talking hurriedly about something. He has one of the most impenetrable accents to come out of Mississippi. J.D. was easier to follow, but he usually sat with a half smile, fanning himself with his hat, listening to what Joe was saying. It was Joe, too, who was always arranging things, trying to get sessions going, trying to get a job together. He was always playing in one of the clubs or dance halls — earning a few dollars a night and keeping himself going on it. J.D. was a partially disabled World War II veteran, and he had a small pension. He had trouble doing a lot of walking, but otherwise he could live a normal life. He didn't have Joe's raw determination to keep going, and often during those years — despite the small audience he had in the colleges — this was all Joe

24

did have. The two of them — Mississippi bluesmen still playing in the old field holler rhythms and half-picking, half-strumming their battered old guitars — were as out of place in the St. Louis of the 1950's as a Model A truck on a Los Angeles freeway. 'But I got a little something going,' Joe would say, and he always did; and J.D would smile and sit waiting until Joe told us what it was.

Crawford, Mississippi isn't much of a town — just a clump of buildings in the low hills of northeastern Mississippi. But after all his years of wandering it's the only place Big Joe Williams thinks of as home, and it's the place he's finally come back to. He didn't have much of anything out of his years of playing until the blues revival of the 1960's. He'd show up in St. Louis or Chicago, stay around a few months doing whatever jobs he could find, then he'd go off again. Bob Koester, who owns the blues and jazz label Delmark Records, did more than anyone else to keep Big Joe going. If I'd come into Chicago when Big Joe was in town I'd usually find him sitting in the back of Bob's shop, getting his business together over the telephone or waiting for somebody to talk to about some new idea he had about making a record or doing a job. But the jobs started paying better, there got to be more of them, and he was finally able to settle — and it was Mississippi, and his old town of Crawford, that he came back to settle in.

Joe was born outside of Crawford in his family's cabin near the Knoxford Swamp, in 1903, on October 16. He was the first child, the first of sixteen; eight boys and eight girls. His mother, Cora Lee Williams, was thirteen when he was born. He's often said that he has some Cherokee blood, and his father, John Williams, was called 'Red Bone'. Some of this is still in his face. Writing about him when he was in his sixties, Charles Edward Smith said, 'His facial expressions change swiftly — reminding one of his lightning-like phrasing of long blues lines — and might shift in a split second from a guileless, completely ingenuous smile, to a look of cynical sadness. Not masks, but the weathering of years. . .'

The music, just as with most of the other country bluesmen, started early. His grandfather, Bert Logan, played the accordian, and he sang songs — most of them play songs, but one of them was the blues that Joe remembers as Crow Jane. Sometimes he remembers making it up himself, but probably he just made up the words to the old melody. The woman was Jane Tripley, from the neighborhood. ' . . . She was a good looking woman when I was a child, still is.' He had cousins that played, one of them a blues guitarist, another a washboard player. His own first instruments were home-made — children's flutes made out of cane reeds, and single string guitars. He made his first one when he was four. The first songs were from his mother and father and grandfather, but he was making up his own blues when he came into his teens.

At the same time, he was beginning to drift. It was during the First World War, and he was one of thousands of young black men who were trying to get away from the desperate life of poverty and anger that they'd known in the poor sharecroppers' cabins. When the United States finally went into the war in 1917 there were job openings in the northern cities and this started people moving. The efforts to stop the move by the Mississippi whites were violent, brutal, and bloody. Men were beaten, some of them lynched — usually burned alive — just for trying to break out of the system that held them down. Even the newspapers reported some of it, and the stories went on week after week. Joe moved, but he stayed close. It was the only life he knew how to deal with. In the beginning he was working the camps along the levees and the railroads, living in tents and dirty shacks, singing for the drunken dances that the companies set up for the men on Saturday nights. The work was ferocious, twelve to sixteen hours a day, depending on the time of year. It was what Big Bill

Broonzy called 'can to can't'. You had to work from when there was enough light so you could see — until it had gotten so dark you couldn't. The pay was as bad as the living conditions and the work — $1.00 or $1.50 a day. The companies brought in women for the dances, and between the women, the liquor — also from the company — and the long night's gambling, nobody ever had any money to show for their relentless labor. Only hard-muscled bodies, and an anger under the skin that never let them rest. Once in a while the anger would come out — someone would go after a boss — but the Mississippi system was too much to take on single-handed, so they took out the anger on each other.

Son House also remembered those same wild Saturday night dances, 'balls', as he called them — the killings, the fights, the raw, bleeding tension behind the sounds of the music and the dancing. He remembered, as well, the conditions that were forcing them out, forcing them to the work gangs on the river, or onto the big plantations.

'At that time there was mostly farm work, and sometimes it got pretty critical. Low wages and . . . well, people kind of suffered a little during some of those years. Suffered right smart. In some places they got a little better than they did in others. But they stayed up against it mostly. Bad housing and all that kind of stuff. Of course, they'd get plenty of just old common food, but they didn't make enough money to do any good. Some of those that grew crops — if they paid their debts for the food they ate during the year, why, if they came out and cleared as much as forty or fifty dollars for a year, they were satisfied. Out of a whole year's work! Of course, along then, they didn't see into it too much because they'd been used to it for so long. . . .'

Joe was able to get out of the camps to play in the road houses and at country picnics, and he was doing mostly what he felt like. He was in Alabama for awhile in the 1920's, playing for a man named Totsie King in

27

Tuscaloosa, who was running the local rackets in the Tuscaloosa poor section, 'the M & O Bottoms'. He was in West Helena, Arkansas, for awhile, playing for the workers at the lumber mill there. He lived as hard as the men he was playing for — drinking, going after the women, getting shot at, getting his guitars broken. It was during this loose, drifting part of his life that he started making over the guitars he was playing. He bought broken instruments and added strings, doubling first the top, then the second string, then the fourth string. Usually he screwed another set of pegs across the top of the peg box and ran the strings down from there. He left the third string single so he could get more out of the string with the 'choked' tones that are part of the Mississippi style. The doubled strings gave him his own distinctive, rasping sound.

For men like Joe — and J.D. — so much happened to them, and they drifted so far, that their lives begin to take on the quality of a dream. Even Joe himself has a difficult time keeping all of it straight. He was with a medicine show for awhile — in a jug band with the Rabbit's Foot Minstrels. He thinks they made some records for OKeh in Atlanta in 1928, but the records have never been found. He says he did some blues for Paramount Records in Chicago in 1931, under the name King Solomon Hill, but the singer on the records isn't Big Joe. In the first years of the Depression he went back to the levee gangs, even working on the W.P.A for awhile. It does seem that he did one session in the studio in the twenties — for Vocalion in the Peabody Hotel in Memphis in September, 1929 — but his career as a recording artist began in Chicago in 1935. He did six songs for Bluebird on February 25. Later the same year, in October, he recorded again, and the first song was 'Baby Please Don't Go'. It was probably something he'd heard before, but he was able to copyright it as his own composition, and it's been this, almost as much as the singing, that helped get him his house in Crawford. He went on recording — by himself, with other musicians, doing all kinds of blues — just as he goes on now, the music seeming to burst out of the harsh Mississippi life that shaped it.

'. . . It's a lot of times we can get very worried and dissatisfied, and we can get to singing the blues, and if we can play music and play the blues we may play the blues for awhile until we get kind of pacified. That cuts off a lot of worry.'

J.D. Short was sitting in his kitchen in the summer of 1962, talking about his blues. The legacy of the blues that Big Joe and J.D. sang was their directness as a language, a kind of directness that insisted on the blues as an immediate voice. It has been one of the most important of the things that blues has given to the black society — a song form that was part of spoken speech, that was immediately involved with experience. Much of the blues can be limited and repetitive, but the older Mississippi men used it as they used talking — to say something. It had been so long since popular song in the United States had said anything directly and openly that the effect was startling. It was this openness, as much as anything else, that forced American popular music to change so completely in the 1960's.

J.D. was so quiet, so careful of what he said, that it was always a sudden surprise when he began to sing. His voice was heavy and powerful, with a kind of throbbing vibrato that he did with his mouth and lips. He was so strong a singer that the guitar had to plunge after the voice in a relentless rush. He usually had a metal rack clamped on to the body of his guitar with one or two harmonicas in it, and his harmonica playing was a quiet, lyric contrast to the voice and the guitar. The first time he sang for me was in a shadowed room up over Delmark Avenue in St. Louis, singing only for his wife and myself as the sun went down over the shabby street and the last Saturday traffic made its way over the rough paving. Footsteps had been moving on the stairs outside, voices in the kitchens and bedrooms around us in the building, but as he sang the other voices gradually stopped, and there was finally only J.D.

Like Joe, he was born out of the delta — but to the south of it, in the quiet, small town of Port Gibson. As a town it still looks as it must have looked sixty or seventy years ago; brick buildings lining a business street, frame houses back on the side streets, the fields of the surrounding farms backing up against the garages and the warehouses of the main street. He was older than his cousin by almost a year. He was born in Port Gibson on December 26, 1902. His family was working poor farms, drifting from one town to another. When he was seven, in 1909, they began moving toward the north, staying for times in places like Hollandale and Sholes, Mississippi. From 1912 to 1923 the family was mostly in Clarksdale, which was the delta blues country, and it was in the delta that J.D. learned most of his early music. A man named Willie Johnson taught him some things in Hollandale; he learned some piano from Son Harris in Sholes. He saw Charley Patton when Charley stopped by their cabin in Mirthy Bow — outside of Hollandale — and played the guitar J.D.'s father had hanging up on the wall.

Big Joe had been moving around some of the same country, but J.D. decided he couldn't stay. He felt the same brooding need to get out — to leave Mississippi behind. All of it pivoted on the pitifully low wages that Mississippi whites were forcing the blacks to accept. This had been the reason behind the wave of white violence that had risen after the move out of the state had started. Son House could also remember some of the excitement of it.

'After they commenced waking up, some started going different places and came back with the news that they were doing so much better. "Up in such-and-such-a-place, they pay so-much-and-so-much. That what I make." Well, that wakes the other guys up. He sees his old buddy all dressed up and looking so nice, and so they comment from one to another and commence to easing out to these different places. If they get as far as St. Louis, oh Jesus! They thought they was somewhere.

I did it myself! I had a friend who was up there working in the Commonwealth Steel Plant in St. Louis. He came back and was telling me about it, and the first thing you know, I'd sneaked out and gone to St. Louis. We were getting a dollar an hour along then. That was big money, you know. That was way back yonder. A dollar an hour! Whooo! That was along in 1922 or '23. The Commonwealth Steel Plant. . . .'

J.D. could even remember the day he'd come up to St. Louis; April 16, 1923. He got a job at Mueller's Brass Foundry, and that's where he stayed, keeping his blues for the nights and the weekends. Mississippi had become his past.

There was a lot of blues in St. Louis in the 1920's — from Lonnie Johnson to Victoria Spivey, and mostly through the efforts of Jessie Stone, who was scouting for OKeh records and running a record shop that all the singers dropped into; nearly everyone got to record. J.D. was part of two groups of St. Louis musicians that left on recording trips. In late 1930 he went up to Chicago with Alice Moore, Henry Brown, and some other singers to record for Paramount. He did four songs that were among the last things Paramount released, under the name Jaydee Short. Two years later he was in New York, probably with Peetie Wheatstraw, to do four songs for Vocalion as Jelly Jaw Short. After that he left the blues for a few years, playing clarinet in Douglas Williams' big swing band. This kind of isolation from the commercial side of the blues is what kept his music so unchanged — that kept it so important as a document of the earlier delta blues styles.

His last trip out of St. Louis had little to do with music. He'd always looked young, and in 1942, at the age of forty, he got into the army and began training with the 92nd Division. Six months later, in March,

1943, he was injured on an obstacle course and discharged. The injury never healed completely. When I first met him he'd had two toes amputated — three or four months after we'd recorded together for the last time he died in his bed in the small house he and his wife were renting on one of the littered back streets of the St. Louis ghetto.

Just as it was impossible for people to go past J.D.'s door in St. Louis that late afternoon when I first heard him sing, it was impossible not to see Big Joe and his cousin. It was impossible not to get some disturbing glimpse of the life they'd been through. They were visible men. It isn't enough to say that the legacy they gave us was the directness of the language and the insistent honesty of the emotions in what they sang. The most important legacy of these two hard, worn men — and from other bluesmen like them — was that they made us *see* them; and for a black man in America that has turned out to be the most difficult of all the things he has had to go through.

Bukka White

Bukka White

AN INNER SENSE OF SELF
- Bukka White

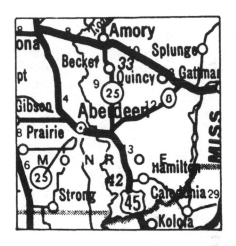

'Bluesman.' To define it as someone who sings the blues is too narrow. It's true, but it only defines one dimension, one aspect of the blues. To define it as someone who responds to his life, to his environment, in terms of the artistic language known as the blues comes closer to it. Closer — and at the same time suggests some of the music's larger dimensions. One of the most important functions of the blues is this act of self-definition, and it's this that gives the blues its validity as language — as the language of the black culture in America.

To someone involved with the blues as an integral part of his life the music was a clarification of the realities of his experience. The language itself was an expression of the shared reality of an entire culture, and the bluesman's definition of the reality became a way to objectify the experience, to somehow keep it at a distance. Sometimes, when you talk with Bukka White, you feel that the blues he sings *are* the reality — or at least they're as close to it as he can come. In his late sixties now, a lot of his time is spent talking about his life, and the blues he's woven out of it are part of the memory he has of it. He's set up three or four wooden seats and an old bench against a brick wall not far from his apartment in Memphis, and he spends his mornings there talking. He calls it his 'office', where he 'does his business'. The business, now, is remembering the things that have happened to him, and as he tells you something about his life in 1934, or someone he knew in 1937, some of it comes out in blues phrases — in verses from the blues he wrote about it. There's no place for him where the two are separate.

Bukka comes from the same part of Mississippi as Big Joe Williams, the hill country east of the delta, going over toward the Alabama border. In the early thirties, just after he got married, he was farming about twenty miles from Joe's town of Crawford, north on what is now Alternate Route 45 to the even smaller town of West Point. Sometimes he's said his birthdate was in 1906, other times 1909; but the day is definite, November 12. His father was named John White, a fireman on the M & O Railroad, originally from Texas, but settled in Houston, Mississippi, when he married Lula Davis and started his family. They were living on the farm of his mother's father when Booker was born — Booker T. Washington White, named for the black leader who took the first steps after the Civil War to force some recognition of black rights on a hostile

36

white society. Booker, as his name probably should be spelled, though he's always known as Bukka, was one of five children. They were living east of Clarksdale and the other delta towns — about ninety miles from Clarksdale — and without a car and on the back country mud roads, the delta was a long way off.

The music began early. His father played guitar and violin, and he took the children to church where they started singing. Both Bukka and his sister Etta were taught how to play a little on the guitar. But Bukka's drifting started early — even earlier than most. When he was nine he went into Houston, Mississippi, and took a job in a lumber yard. The family came and got him, but when he was fourteen he went off to live with his uncle in Grenada, Mississippi, outside of Clarksdale. He was already playing the guitar and singing a little when he ran off from Clarksdale and got as far as St. Louis. He says that he painted on a moustache and did well in the honky tonks playing for the 'pretty girls'. He had to get back to Clarksdale and he remembers that sometime during his time there there was trouble with his uncle over the music. There was a piano in the house, both for Bukka and for his uncle's son Buster, but Bukka was interested in the guitar and he had an old instrument that was patched up but still playable. He tried to play it late at night when he thought everybody would be asleep, but he woke up the house once too often and his uncle destroyed the guitar.

The drifting that started then in his life still goes on. As he says, 'I like to talk and have a good time — like a fish — take him out of water and lay him on the bank in the hot sun and he'll soon dry up and die — that's the way I am — if you don't put me someplace where I can have fun, I won't like it long.' But he finished his teens working on the farm with his uncle or carrying water for construction gangs. He stayed with the music — even then it was giving some direction to his casual days. It was about the only thing he had. He hadn't bothered with school — he'd mostly just worked on the farms or helped with the construction gangs. It was about as much education as most other young black men in Mississippi got in the early 1920's, and it wasn't enough to break the cycle of tenant farm laboring that shaped their lives.

But Bukka could sing, and he was already a brilliant guitarist, with a kind of drumming, frailed style; a surging, rhythmic background to his dark voice. By the time he was in his early twenties he was ready to do something with his music. The first recordings were for a scout for Victor Records, Ralph Limbo, who was running a furniture store in Ita Bena. The man who was responsible for Victor's blues recordings, Ralph Peer, had already learned that local people had a much better knowledge of the artists and their sales potential than he did, so for recordings of this kind he let his scouts have considerable freedom. Depending on which birth date is correct Bukka was either twenty or twenty-three when Limbo told him he'd take him up to Memphis for a recording session in late May, 1930. He told Bukka to meet him 'at the railroad tracks at Swann Lake', on Monday morning, May 26, and Bukka still can remember that he was so excited he was there waiting every morning for a week before he was supposed to meet him.

After four or five sessions in the studio nobody remembers the details so clearly — it all becomes part of the life of a working musician. Jobs, rehearsals, recordings. They're all part of what he does. If it's a good session, something coming together in a new way — then people remember what happened; they remember the names of who they were with, what songs they were working on. But after a time the hours in the studio lose their sharp distinctiveness. Only the first session is never really forgotten. Everybody can remember what it was like to sit down in front of a microphone for the first time. Bukka still remembers everything about that first day in Memphis. The car Limbo was driving was a new Studebaker, and he had four other artists with him when he drove up; two white guitar players, a black preacher, and a blues singer named Napoleon Hairiston. When the session started Bukka and Hairiston worked together, the two of them doing fourteen of the sixteen sides that Limbo had contracted to do with his black artists. Hairiston actually played and sang on only five of the songs, and of these only one was issued, the first thing they recorded, 'The New 'Frisco Train'. Bukka did a brilliant train piece, spoken against a rushing guitar background, 'The Panama Limited', that was issued with the duet with Hairiston. The blues he did were never issued, which was unfortunate, since he had to wait seven years for the chance to record blues again. He did 'The Doctor Blues', 'Mississippi Milk Blues', 'Women Shootin' Blues', and 'Mule Lopin' Blues', and he and Hairiston did four blues duets: 'Stranger Woman Blues', 'Jealous Man Blues', 'Mama Ain't Goin' To Have It Here', and 'Dirty Mistreatin' Blues'. He doesn't remember any of them — though verses or melodies may still turn up in pieces he does today.

The blues weren't as popular in 1930 as they had been two or three years earlier — the Depression had a lot to do with it, and there had also been a lot of blues records released. Probably because of this Limbo also had him do four religious songs: 'Over Yonder', 'I Am In The Heavenly Way', 'Trusting In My Saviour', and 'Promise True and Grand'. In the Chicago *Defender*, the black newspaper that was the closest thing to a voice that black Americans had during these years, there was an advertisement for Bukka as a religious singer on October 11, 1930. The drawing for the ad used the Noah theme for 'A Promise True and Grand'. Noah was on the deck of the ark with his arms raised toward the heavens, the ark anchored to a shore with flowers, fields, and a flock of goats. Bukka had become 'Washington White, The Singing Preacher'. With some assistance from one of the two men who found him in Memphis thirty-three years later he was able to remember and record it again. Neither of the records that were issued seem to have attracted much attention, and in the confusion of the early years of the thirties Bukka drifted back to his farm life in Mississippi.

He married a woman named Nancy Buchauney in 1933, and moved to a farm in West Point. His wife's uncle was also a blues singer, George 'Bullet' Williams, a Paramount artist who'd done a session in 1928. They worked together outside of West Point the next year; then in 1935 he moved again, about twenty miles north to Aberdeen. He was living there when he got into trouble two years later.

Nearly forty years after Bukka is as offhand about the incident that put him in Parchman Farm as he is about the years in Parchman themselves. He shrugs at a question about it.

'All the girls was wild about me, you know, and one of the girls that really was likin' me — well, her boyfriend wasn't so used to girl friends. He was a young boy; I was older than he was. And the woman he was going with — she was older than he was, she was my age. So, I think I was just a little too famous with the girls.'

All of this was in the small Mississippi town of Prairie, not far from Aberdeen.

'When I came from Aberdeen that evening I was goin' back west to play for my cousin, a dance that night. A cousin named Buck Davidson. See, my mother was a Davidson before she married a White. When I got to Prairie a friend of mine said, "Booker," he say, "you feel just as close to me as a brother of mine 'cause you don't bother nobody. Nobody can't say nothin' about you but they tellin' a lie." Said, "But don't you play your guitar on the street today. They're layin' here for you." I said, "Layin' here for me for what?" He said, "I done told you a long time ago all these women goin' for you. They want to get you out of the way." But they didn't know I had that .38 Colt automatic with the holster right in there in my pocket. I said, "Well, I don't bother them, but if they get ready I'm just as ready to go to their funeral as

they are to go to mine." So that's what happened.'
Bukka points back to the old painted brick wall of a grocery store close to his apartment.

'Just like you see that store right there, there's about fifteen of them linin' up and down there. I'm goin' to get on old man Curley Allen's log truck goin' back west. Me and my friend Russ Quinn, we goin' to that dance over there. But they didn't let me get to the truck. They sent this girl's little boy friend out to start it. Well, he made a slow start . . .'

Bukka shot him in the leg, and he was convicted of assault and sentenced to two years in Parchman. His only bitterness is toward the men who testified against him, saying that he'd picked the fight. 'They railroaded me. There was one of those men — I'd have killed him when I got out, but he was dead already.' He did have a few weeks when he was out on bond, and he used the time to get up to Chicago and do a session with Lester Melrose, who was in charge of blues recording for the American Recording Corporation. He only did two songs at a single session on September 2; 'Pinebluff, Arkansas' and 'Shake 'Em On Down'. Melrose released them during the winter on A.R.C.'s Vocalion label.

How bad was it for him in Parchman Farm? Other men who have been penned in it only remember the harshness, the destructiveness of its endless labor, but it was — when it was first opened — considered to be a model prison. Prison authorities from every part of the United States and Europe either went to look at it or read articles about it. Women were allowed in — there were cabins set up on the grounds for men and women to be alone for the day, and it wasn't necessary that she be a wife. It was a work camp, but the produce was sold and there was a careful accounting kept of the profit and loss of the farm's operation. Most of the work was the same kind of cotton culture the prisoners had known from childhood, so it wasn't that different from the kind of work they'd been doing all their lives. But they were penned there, and they had no share in the profits their labor produced; there was no clear effort made to break the cycle of poverty and illiteracy that had helped get them into Parchman — and they worked in a kind of dull monotony, out in the fields or into the prison workshops, with nothing much to keep them going except the weekend women to look forward to. For someone like Bukka there was something else — his blues. There was music in the prison — singing while the gangs worked in the fields, and music when they'd gotten back in at night. As one of the camp musicians Bukka's life was considerably easier than the others'.

'I carried myself in a way for everybody to like me, but I don't care who you are, white or black or red or brown, sometime people'll make you do things you wouldn't think you'd ever come to do. Now I always been good, but I never been no pushover, and so they treated me just like I treat myself. I had a nice time. I played music, they didn't 'low me to work too hard, never got a lick, treated just like I was in the edge of Heaven. That's the way they treated me. Nobody couldn't get me until the time was out. Peoples all over the United States was there, but they couldn't do no good. They wouldn't let the man loose me. They say, "He too much value to the state. We goin' keep him. And don't need nobody else comin' by 'cause you ain't goin' get him." And I made myself happy. I seed I couldn't move; so I played them blues, that's all I was doin'.'

It was at Parchman that Bukka did his third group of recordings; though it wasn't a commercial session. Alan Lomax came to the prison with portable recording equipment to gather material for the Library of Congress folk music archives on May 24, 1939. Bukka remembers, 'I was in there when Mr. Lomax came by and I figured it was better to give than to receive and so I did some numbers for him.' He did two songs, 'Sic 'Em Dogs On', and 'Po' Boy'. 'Po' Boy' is the same song he plays now as 'Poor Boy Long Way From Home'.

When he first talked about his life after his re-discovery he gave the impression that Lester Melrose had been able to get him out of Parchman, but he says now that he had to serve the full two years, and Melrose sent him a train ticket as soon as he was out. Two friends, a slide player named Bob Stovall and someone named Will, had a new car; so they drove up and he gave the ticket back. On Thursday, March 7, and Friday, March 8, 1940, he did two sessions, working with a washboard player that he thinks was probably George Washington. Bukka did twelve songs, some of them with things drawn from his experiences in Parchman, but most of them coming out of the concerns and the involvements of his life in Mississippi. The strongest effect Parchman seems to have had on his blues was to tighten them, and to clarify them, as he worked over his songs and wrote them down so he'd be ready to record when he got out. In the study of these blues in *The Bluesmen* too much emphasis was put on the sombre undertone in the songs that seemed to be shadowed by the years he was there. Many of them, in fact, had been written before he went in.

His most famous blues, 'Fixin' To Die', was an anguished response to the death of his mother. 'High Fever Blues' was about the death of a woman he loved when he was a young man. He still remembers writing the song.

'I writ that "High Fever" 'cause when she died I went to see her that Monday night, she had it. I thought it was the yellow jaundice. She wanted me to play. I said, "Mary, I'm writin' a song," and I said, "What I have written I can play what I know about it and I'll sing it." And so Miss Lucy, that's her mother, she said, "Well, I don't think it would be right for you to play for her, sick as she is, she might get up." And Mary said, "Well, if I get up or don't get up, what goin' do?" And I just went on and played it. Now that was Monday night, and I went back over there Wednesday night to see her, and she was layin' in her casket. I didn't know about it. It hurt me so bad I

43

taken the scarf around my neck and put it around her neck in the casket and walked on out.'

The other songs from the sessions have this same obsessive concern with the moments of his life. The blues that most completely mirrored his Parchman days was the relentless 'When Can I Change My Clothes', as the singer looks down at his prison stripes and wonders, over and over, when he can change them for his civilian clothes. The twelve blues were a hard, unyielding personal summation of what life had given him — both in its good moments and its bad. But they were released in 1940, when the country was beginning to shake off the Depression, and the mood of the Thirties was beginning to change. They weren't much of a success, and after a few months of scuffling he finally settled in Memphis. The recordings were, however, a kind of marking of what he'd been through, and they were finally to lead to his new career twenty-three years later.

In a way it was as if Bukka's blues pursued him through the long years he lived in Memphis in obscurity. He went on with his life, moving from city to city to work odd jobs, but usually coming back to Memphis after a few months — still carrying a guitar with him — working little clubs when he could scuffle up a job. He started to settle down a little, and a daughter, Irene, was born in 1944; then his wife died of ptomaine poisoning on a trip back to Mississippi in 1946, and he went back to his life of lonely rented rooms. He remembers working as a rhythm guitarist in an electric blues band in the early 1950's, and sometimes he saw B.B. King, a younger cousin, when B.B. was just beginning his own career as a bluesman in Memphis. Bukka had a day job in a factory that manufactured metal tanks and lived most of the time in a room on Orleans Street, not far from Beale Street.

But once something gets on to a record it begins to have a life of its own, and Bukka's blues were trailing after him. In 1959 *The Country Blues* was published, with a discussion of his records and the words for

'Fixin' To Die Blues'. In 1963 a letter to Avalon, Mississippi, led to the re-discovery of Mississippi John Hurt, and in 1964 John Fahey, still a student then, though already a startling and enigmatic guitarist, sent a letter to 'Booker T. Washington White (Old Blues Singer), c/o General Delivery, Aberdeen, Mississippi.' One of the blues from the 1940 session had been 'Aberdeen Mississippi Blues'.

I was over in Aberdeen on my way to New Orleans,
I was over in Aberdeen on my way to New Orleans,
Them Aberdeen women told me would buy my gasoline .

There were still relatives in Aberdeen; they sent the letter on to Bukka in Memphis, and he answered Fahey a month later. From *The Bluesmen:*

Two hours after his letter reached Berkeley, Fahey and another blues enthusiast who was a graduate student at the University, Ed Denson, left for Memphis. They found him in his rooming house, found that he still played, recorded him that first afternoon, and a few weeks later released a long playing record of the session.

There had always been a feeling of strength in Bukka's recordings, and the new material made it clear that the strength had grown from his belief in his music. There had been almost no change in style in the thirty-five years that had passed since he began recording. There had been a slight easing of the harshness of his singing for the 1937 A.R.C. session, a suggestion of the popular style of Big Bill Broonzy in the phrasing, and there was a second guitar to soften the sound of his delta open tuning. But in 1964 he was just as he had been in 1930, 1939, and 1940. . .'

The kind of big commercial success that Bukka had dreamed of never materialized, despite the recording Fahey and Denson did of him. There was even a 45 rpm single, 'World Boogie' and 'Midnight Blues', but the copies never sold very well and for years the singles sat in boxes under the clothes piled on the floor of the closet in Ed's back garden Berkeley cottage. Bukka came out to California, and there were a few months of coffee house jobs, but the work dwindled and he finally went back to Memphis. There was some disappointment for him that it didn't all come to more, but he has a steady stream of jobs at festivals and colleges — and despite the difficulty of getting to the small, straggling street where he lives people come by to talk to him about the old days and ask him about guitar pickings. He married again in 1964, and he and his new wife, Leola, have three children. His life is quiet, but full, and he has hours to talk with the friends who stop by the 'office' for a morning. He talks excitedly, one hand on his knee as he leans forward to point with the other. The things he describes are the same things he sings about — the blues simply part of his language — another, natural way for him to speak.

Robert Pete Williams

Robert Pete Williams

' YOU CAN HEAR THE SOUND OF IT, COMIN ' FORTH SOUNDIN ' GOOD '

- Robert Pete Williams

It had been raining for three days in southern Louisiana — a cold, persistent rain that overflowed the shallow ditches beside the roads and seeped across the uneven streets and narrow sidewalks of the small towns. In front of some of the houses there were small lakes where the gardens had been, and around little crossroad grocery stores the water backed up in broad ripples whenever a car drove past. In a small group of houses outside the town of Rosedale — not far from Louisiana's capitol, Baton Rouge — the water streamed in dark rivulets off the raised hump of the tarred road and washed against the front steps of the small, one-storey houses. A school bus had just emptied at one end of the street, its pent-up noise of voices and laughter spilling out across the neighborhood as the students — mostly adolescents — splashed through the puddles on their way home. In a house in the middle of the block a strong, dark, quiet man was sitting on a couch close to the front window watching for his own children. His house wasn't much different from any of the others in the neighborhood, and he didn't look much different from the people passing along in the street, but there was a guitar on the couch beside him and some picks and strings spread out on a low table. It was the house of one of the few country bluesmen still living and performing in the South. A poster from a concert was tacked to the wall next to the bedroom door. His name was printed across it, 'Robert Pete Williams'.

His daughters came into the room, piling books on the table, getting themselves bread and butter, telling him the day's excitements and confusions. His wife, Hattie Mae, was in the kitchen, standing at the stove fixing supper. Robert Pete was listening to them, answering them, but his mind was somewhere else. A recording session had been scheduled for later in the evening in Baton Rouge, and after two days of talking and thinking about material he was beginning to withdraw into a silent, nervous mood. It was just the same as being in a room with any creative artist in any medium — a painter, a poet, a composer — when an idea comes into his mind and he begins working with it. Instead of talking he began to look away, out of the window, and when he did say something it was slow and abstracted, most of his mind on the images of the blues he was going to sing.

Robert Pete has spent his life as a laborer, and he's still solidly built; a short, strong man with a large chest and shoulders. He'd changed out of his work clothes into the costume he wears when he's performing; striped, flared trousers and polished high-heeled boots, a short-sleeved sport shirt and a broad-brimmed Stetson hat that sits at an angle off his forehead. He stood at the kitchen table with a cup of coffee in his hand. He has high blood pressure now and he has to watch his diet. As he says, 'I talk it over with Hattie Mae now I'm gettin' old and she say all that's comin' down on you from when you were young.'

Hattie Mae had cooked a big supper — collard greens and neck bones, fried gar fish, and mashed potatoes with bits of pickle mixed in. Everyone ate except Robert Pete, who took a little fish, finished his coffee, and went to put his guitar in its case. A pint of vodka went into the case with it. He doesn't drink much when he's in the house, but it helps loosen his fingers, and his imagination, when he's performing. He moved restlessly around the room, went and stood looking out the door. Friends passing called to him, and he nodded; then turned back to look at the clock. We finished supper, Hattie Mae put away the dishes, and it was time to go to Baton Rouge.

Robert Pete's first recordings were done at the state prison farm at Angola, Louisiana, by Dr Harry Oster in 1959. Oster, a professor of English at Louisiana State University, was recording the music of all of Louisiana's cultural groups, and he'd gone into Angola to record the work gang songs still sung there. He found these, and he also found three bluesmen, Hogman Maxey, Guitar Welch, and Robert Pete Williams. Robert Pete was not only the most exciting of the three, he was one of the most exciting bluesmen to be found in years. It wasn't only the intensity of his music — it was the spontaneous, almost free creativity of his blues that was so individual. As he described it to Oster,

'All the music I play, I just hear it in the air. You can hear the sound of it, comin' forth, soundin' good. Well, all of my blues that I put out, that was made up

51

blues. I make up my own blues you see. Why, I may be walkin' along or ridin' in a car and blues come to me, and I just get it all in my head. Well, I come back and I get my guitar and then I play it.'

After almost fifteen years of playing and recording, his blues still come to him 'in the air'. He has themes, obsessions, that come back to him again and again, but his songs are always changing, always newly shaping themselves. He is almost, in himself, a definition of the country bluesman — a poet of his own experience, his language and idiom coming from the hard country background that shaped him. To be with him when he's recording is like sharing the experience of his blues.

He was born on March 14, 1914 in Zachary, Louisiana, another small town not far from Baton Rouge, where his father had a small farm. It was a poor, hard life, and when he was still a boy he was already working for somebody else.

'I was in my teen-age when I started. I slept in the barn and I laid on sacks and I laid under sacks. I'd get a cup of coffee and a piece of bread for breakfast. When I'd see the light burning in the kitchen I'd be like a dog. I'd know I was getting food. All of that for $12 a month.'

When he was fourteen he was working in a lumberyard in Scotlandville, another small town not far from where he lives now. He made himself a guitar when he was twenty, learned a little on it, and finally bought a real one. But it wasn't the blues that he was drawn to first. He told Oster,

'Music begin to follow me then. I been trying to stop playing music, thinking about lookin' out for preparing my soul for Jesus. I was a Christian man before I got here. I can play church songs too, just as well as I can blues. What Jesus gave me, He didn't take it away from me. He sent me to be a preacher and I didn't like it . . .'

For the next twenty years his life was poor and uncertain, but there were wives, children — 'I got me eight head of boys' — and he didn't stop living. There were jobs, Sundays when he slept late and Saturday nights when he stayed up late. He was at the Curry Lumber Company for a long time, stacking lumber for 75c an hour. He was living in Port Allen with a woman named Dora Lee and their four children. After that he worked at the Standard Oil coopering shop, cleaning metal barrels with caustic soda. He still has scars from acid burns he got working with the barrels. He had his day jobs, and he had the night jobs when he played a little guitar and sang.

It wasn't until he was forty-two that Robert Pete's life fell to pieces. Early in 1956 he killed a man in a ramshackle bar called Bradley's Club in Scotlandville. At his trial he claimed it was self-defence, and he still has a clear, tormenting memory of what happened to him that day.

'I come to the bar and there was these two fellows there, one with his head back, leanin', and the other one, a big man, and I was standin' there and he says, "Where you from?" and I say "Zachary," and he says "You lyin'," and I says, "No, I'm from Zachary," and I got myself a quart of beer and I went over to a table with it to drink there with some boys I knew and after a minute the big one comes after me again, sayin' something, and I gets up, and he says to the one leanin' "I'm goin' take care of this . . ." and grabs my arm, grabs the sleeve, and I pulls away. I'm just small and I didn't want to fight him. I could of got away but the door done got blocked, you know, all the people who'd come up around to see like they do in a fight. He had a knife, a duckbill kind of knife with a broad blade and he come at me. I had the gun. That's the truth. I did have it. But Scotlandville's a bad place, they got men that won't stop anything they's doin'. If I was to go there today I'd carry a gun. So he come at me and I shot him. In the stomach. But you know, he didn't go down, and it was a .45 I shot him with. He just stumbled over a little and leaned on a table, then he started to come at me again.

You know if you hit a man with a .45 and he don't go down he's strong — so I shot him again in the heart.'

At the trial he says there were no witnesses for him. The people who'd been in the club weren't going to come to the police for somebody who wasn't from the town, even if it was somebody they knew. Without witnesses to the fight — the police couldn't find the knife and the other man had been shot twice with a .45 — Robert Pete didn't have much of a chance. He was sentenced to life imprisonment, and he went into Angola to begin serving his sentence on April 6, 1956.

He tried, from the beginning, to get out. When Oster found him in the prison three years later he'd already made three efforts to get paroled, only to be turned down each time. He didn't give up the music, though there was a shortage of instruments, and they had to pass around what they had. When Oster came through the wire gates with his recording equipment Robert Pete was ready. He still remembers how hard it was to bring himself to play.

'It was so hard to play when Dr. Oster came there — everybody was so close and standing behind you and you gets so nervous. Some of them men look like they could eat barbed wire and sleep sound all night.'

But he played. Oster and other people began to work to get him out, writing to Louisiana's governor, Earl Long. Their appeals were successful and he was freed on December 1, 1959, but it was a conditional freedom and he was technically a parolee to be held in the custody of a white farmer with land outside of Denham Springs, Louisiana. He was kept almost as a field slave — the small salary he got the only difference between what he had to endure and what the men and women before him had to endure before the 1860's. He says about it, with a flare of anger, 'If I had to go back on parole, I'd rather do my time in the penitentiary.'

In the summer of 1964 he was finally free — in time for the Newport Folk Festival. If he was confused at finding himself suddenly in a massed crowd of young whites who were excited at seeing him play, he didn't show any of it. He was in a new suit and a straw hat, talking with anyone who came up to him, but his eyes shifted from face to face as people came close, his own face almost expressionless. And he sang with the same free creativity of the session he'd done for Oster five years before, Newport's loudspeakers blaring his voice and guitar through the gray, damp air over the faces staring back at him.

Rosedale is west of Baton Rouge, on the drier country that lifts out of the swamps below the Mississippi River and New Orleans' Lake Ponchartrain. The land is still flat and muddy, with meandering bayous crossed with small bridges as the roads criss-cross over the weed-choked waters. The house Robert Pete built for himself and Hattie Mae is outside of Rosedale — in a small black community straddling the railroad tracks just beyond a large lumber company where a lot of the men work. He built the house of materials and lumber he found around the countryside as he worked with his own truck picking up scrap metal. It's one-story, painted white, with a small front porch. His truck is usually pulled into a small driveway alongside.

Hattie Mae was driving when it was time to go into the studio, a friend sitting in the car with them. The music has made it possible for Robert Pete to add some things to his life, and their car was new — a big sedan that Hattie Mae drove easily through the darkness. The small back roads opened out onto the double lane highway going into Baton Rouge, then the road lifted up onto the curve of the long bridge over the Mississippi and dropped down into the city. The streets were outlined with lights, glaring with lights, but like most American small cities the night streets were empty. Most of the people have moved out to clutches of suburb at the ends of the road. The few drifters still in the business section were sitting in the movies or in one of the bars, or in a hotel lobby in front of the TV.

Robert Pete has no trouble with studios or microphones now. He was still in his mood of withdrawn concentration, making every motion with the slowness of a man watching himself in a mirror. The bottle of vodka went beside his foot — he spent a lot of time tuning the guitar. The guitar strings didn't need all the time, but he needed it, still getting lines and verses in his head, staring across the studio as he tried out rhythms and fingerings. He uses a slide now. He learned from Fred McDowell, the Mississippi bluesman who was also at Newport when Robert Pete first left the South. They'd become good friends. 'If Fred had a nickel I had a nickel, and if I had a nickel Fred had a nickel.' He got the slide — a piece of metal tubing — out of the guitar case, took a sip of the vodka, then nodded to the engineer, Bill Triche, that he was ready to start.

The blues can be a restricted, tight, idiom, restlessly closed into its three line verse form and repetitive harmonies like a horse wheeling around and around a threshing stone. To break away there has to be a certain individuality, a rough determination to make the form become something more personal. The legacy of the blues of Robert Pete Williams has been their direct responsiveness to what he's thinking, what he's feeling. He uses the blues form — begins with the form, then once it's set up he seems to move easily around it, standing close enough to get back to it if he senses that he's started to drift, but still loose enough with it to use it any way he wants.

Themes persist in his blues, but even the same experience becomes new again when he returns to it. In 1959, when he sang about his imprisonment for Dr. Oster, his dominant concern was understandably his effort to get paroled. In 1973 the emphasis had changed to the trial itself, and his feelings at his sentencing.

Lord, I had a fall, I had a fall in 1955.
Lord, I had a fall, babe, 1955.
The police picked me up, handcuffed me, carried me
to jail.

Locked me down, they tried me for my life,
April the 6th, 1956, they sent me to Angola.
Not to lie, not to lie, they tried me for my life.
Cried, let's keep the poor boy.

You know I called out, you cannot keep me, no, no.
I said I got a man in here in this courthouse with all
power in his hand.
They asked me what man that you talkin' 'bout,
I was lookin dead down at the Bible you know,
I said God above got all power over me.

Yeh, you got to send me to your pen, I ain't thinkin'
'bout your 'lectric chair at all.
Oh you got to send me to your pen, and I'm not be
there long.
Oh yeh, you got to send me to your pen, Lord, I'm
not goin' be there long.

Uuum, Lord.

You know you got the poor boy your way, but that's
alright, that's alright.
One of these ol' days, one of these ol' days,
Lord, I'm goin' walk out this ol' lonesome pen.

You can keep me down in here, but God's got his
eyes on you.
Yeh, you can keep me down in here, but god's got his
eyes on you.

They give me my sentence, natural life.
I say, that's alright, that's alright,
I (take ahead) every time.
But I won't be here long. Just tell me the day will I
stay, 1956.
'59, '59, I was outside with my kids, yeh, Lord . . .

He didn't talk much between songs, still concentrating, still thinking about what he was going to do next. He hardly listened to the occasional playbacks. It was almost as though the blues to him was a 'voice', and not a performance. When he'd finished a song he was like someone who's finished telling a long story. He doesn't want to listen to it again, he wants to get on to something else. Hattie Mae sat on a couch in the control room quietly listening. It was only as he came close to the end of the session that his mood began to lighten. He'd shaken off some of the intensities that had gone into creating the songs. As he stood up to stretch he was smiling, and he had a last sip of the bottle before Hattie Mae came into the studio to wait for him to get his things ready to leave. It was raining again when we got out into the darkness — a light mist of rain blowing across the cars, the bright shine of the lights gleaming over the empty streets.

Robert Pete Williams' blues have come out of the life, the background, that have been his only reality. But like other artists he isn't closed into the reality now. The expression of it has set him outside it. But he doesn't feel himself estranged — the voice that is the blues for him goes on. When he thinks about his own small community he says thoughtfully,
'I don't go out to these little places here to play because you know I got in that little trouble and people think of that and they might get shooting around me and I'd get a bullet. I went out last Christmas and played with a man played, you know, violin, but that was the only time. It's just too rough, those places back on those little roads ...'
But those 'places back on those little roads ...' have been his life, both as a man and as an artist, and they will go on being part of his blues.

Juke Boy Bonner

Juke Boy Bonner

A PARTLY MADE WORLD
- Juke Boy Bonner

My father passed on when I was two years old,
Didn't leave me a thing but a whole lot of soul.
> *You can see I'm a bluesman,*
> *Man, man you know I'm a bluesman.*
I want the whole world to know why I'm a bluesman.
How do you find the dimensions of the world you live in? How do you find what measures it, marks it off? You can find some dimension of your life in the words you use to describe it. In a serious way you measure

yourself by the words you use to describe yourself. 'Bluesman.' The word Juke Boy Bonner uses to describe himself. He means by it a man who makes a living out of singing the blues — the blues as defined in the old dictionaries as '. . . a sad song in a minor key about love sung by the Negro people in America.' But he also means it as something else — as a 'commentor' — a person who comments, who tells.

'Commentor' is probably as close as it's possible to come to the African word 'griot', a word Juke Boy doesn't know, and probably wouldn't even understand, even if he is, in his own haphazard Texas way, one of the singers of blues songs who continues this other traditional role. In a collection of narratives of early African travel printed in London 1745, *Green's Collection of Voyages*, there is a series of references to the griots.

Of the role of the musician in the society there seems to be considerable agreement, although there are differences in the name. 'Those who play on the instruments are persons of a very singular character, and seem to be their poets as well as musicians, not unlike the Bards among the Irish and the ancient Britons. All the French authors, who describe the countries of the Kalofs and Fulis, called them *Guiriots*, but Jobson gives them the name of *Juddies*, which he interprets *fiddlers*. Perhaps the former is the Jalof and Fuli name, the latter, the Mandindo.'

The traveler Barbot says the Guiriot in the language of the Negroes toward the Sanaga, signifies Buffoon, and that they are a sort of sycophant. 'The Kings and great men in the country keep each of them two, or more of these Guiriots to divert them and entertain Foreigners on occasion.'

The necessity of being the buffon — as well as the poet, musician, bard. Juke Boy would recognize all of these roles. And he would recognize something else as well, in the place in the society of the griot.

From *Jobson* 'The fiddlers (guiriots) are reckoned

rich, and their wives have more crystal, blue stones, and beads about them than the king's wives . . . and it is remarkable that after all this fondness of the people for music, and yet the Musician is held in great contempt and is denied their common Rite of Burial, instead of which the Corps is set upright in a hollow tree and left there to rot. The reason they give for this treatment is, that these cantators have a familiar converse with their Devil, Ho-re.' Labat agrees in almost everything with Jobson: He says that the greater part of the Negroes, especially the politer sort, look upon the musicians as infamous, although, being a necessary Tool for their Pleasure, they do not shew it while living: But as soon as they are dead, this contempt appears, since they do not suffer their wives or children to put the corps into the ground . . .

Every bluesman has had to live with the disapproval of what in the 19th Century would have been called the 'politer sort' of the black community. The strong and pervasive religious elements of black life are all hostile to him, and the middle class professionals — school teachers, administrators, businessmen — tend to look at the blues singers as a symbol of the lower class life they've fought so hard to escape. The preachers try to get the bluesmen to give up their blues — and the way of life that goes with the music — and the bluesmen themselves often have to assure people that they can sing gospel songs, too. Like the griots some of the bluesmen have gotten a good living out of it — but like the griots they've had to do without any serious respect for what they've created, or for their role in their society. Even in their old age most of the country bluesmen live in an agonizing isolation, with people living around them almost unconcerned with what they've achieved as artists.

But Juke Boy Bonner goes on as a bluesman, and he goes on with his role of commentor. He insists on forcing the boundaries of the blues to give way, open out, admit more than they're usually expected to admit.

My mother passed on when I was just about eight,
I started to learn I was growin' up in a world of hate,
That made me a bluesman,
You can see why I'm a bluesman.
I want the world to understand what made me
into a bluesman.

As a commentor he says 'world of hate'. It's true, but only a handful of bluesmen have said it — and often they're saying it in Europe, away from the pressure of the American world they have to live in. The next verse goes on with the theme, insisting on the injustice of what happened to him.

I go to work in the fields when I was just thirteen,
Didn't get a chance to know what education means.
I'm a bluesman,
Man, that made me a bluesman.
I want the world to know what it takes to make
a real bluesman.

He could almost be saying that it was anger made him a blues singer. He isn't, since the blues isn't a song form associated with anger — the word for that is the clumsy expression 'protest singer' — but he is associating the term with poverty and rejection. This could be some distant, long-lived reflection of the role of the griot just making its way to the light, despite the centuries it had to be buried under the layers of racism in America. But there is no clear definition of this, and he moves away from this kind of open insistence in the rest of the blues. Most blues are about difficulties with the loved person — man or woman — most of the others are about loneliness. In the last two verses he almost defines the standard themes of the blues.

I growed up and got married, was tryin' to settle down,
The next thing I knew woman tryin' to put me down,
That made me a bluesman,
Man, that made me a bluesman.
Man, tellin' you the truth what it takes to make
a real bluesman.
Lay down at night you don't know where you're
goin' to sleep,

> *Where on earth your next meal to eat,*
> *That make you a bluesman,*
> *Uumh, bluesman.*
> *I want the world to know how come*
> *I'm a bluesman.*

How does someone like Juke Boy Bonner come to be a commentor on his society, instead of someone who is only led through the traces of his life by the society's pressures? As always with a bluesman there isn't much in the background to tell why. It's the usual story of poverty, family instability, near despair, and early flight just to get away — the story of most of the people who are the audience for the bluesman. It's only the occasional individual who pushes his way out of it. Juke Boy was born on a farm in Bellville, Texas, on March 22, 1932. Bellville is in the rolling, dry country west of Houston, in the southeastern part of the state. It's far enough east to still have the heavy rains of winter, but the countryside's beginning to get drier as it gets further toward the west. In the winters the back roads trail through the deep, heavy mud; in the summer there is a smell of dust over the flat fields.

His father, Manuel Bonner, was a sharecropper, with a small patch of land west of Bellville, on state road 159, going toward the even smaller town of Nelsonville. In 1932, when Weldon Bonner — Juke Boy's real name — was born, the rural economy throughout the United States was in a state of collapse. The United States was in the lowest point of the Depression, with banks falling, businesses closing — in some places the cities had to issue their own currency. There were eight other Bonner children — Juke Boy was the youngest — and they were at the lowest end of the economic scale. The family's last chance to stay together ended the next year when, as he said in the blues, 'My father passed on when I was two years old.' The next year Juke Boy was sent to an older family, and the rest of the children were scattered out to friends and relatives. His mother, Cary, died in 1940, '. . . when I was just about eight.'

Few singers have given us such a raw sketch of their own lives. Juke Boy's sketch is rough and unsentimental — a hardness to his voice over the steady shuffle rhythm in the guitar; the harmonica like someone else singing along to the guitar behind him, in the wordless mood of it catching the glint of the songs' depths. 'I go to work in the fields when I was just thirteen/Didn't get a chance to know what education means.' He was thirteen in 1945, and he'd gone to live with one of his older sisters, who already had a family of her own.

The music began at the same time. The money he got for working on the cotton crop went into a guitar that he bought for $3.50. It was years ago, but he still remembers it. He hasn't forgotten anything of those early years — even if there are stretches it's painful to talk about. The first guitar was a beginning, but it was stolen before he'd had it a year. The next one was harder — $12.50 from a store in Bellville, but he was already starting to play out a little. It's hard and poor growing up in the small farm towns of the South, but there's still some sense of community, people still involve themselves with each other. He was too young to play in the clubs, but he had church suppers and private dances to sing to. By the end of 1947, when he was fifteen, he made it out of the farm town to the city of Houston, not many miles to the east.

When you drive into Houston out of the flat, tree covered land around it — crossing the stretches of wet fields — you can see Houston's downtown center of skyscrapers rising over the land, like some vague drawing of the future projected over the drabness of the present. The town's center hangs over the shabby black neighborhoods that ring it. It's a poor town for most of the black men and women trying to get along in it — but it is a center for the back farms. It has some excitements; it has its own world of music and small time crime and petty hustling, all of it going on in the ragged apartment buildings and the house-lined back streets that open windows and doors against the summer heat and stuff clothes around the window frames in the winters.

Anyone working in Houston's music scene finds out soon that one man, Lightnin' Hopkins, 'owns' most of the blues in town. In the '40's and '50's, when his records were coming out regularly and he was working most of the clubs in town, his style left its imprint on everybody. A young musician like Juke Boy was no different, and his music still has a lot of the flavor of Lightnin's even though they're from different generations and hear rhythms in a different way. Juke Boy got into the professional blues world with a local talent show at Houston's Lincoln Theatre, then a short program on a radio station. He was married when he still was very young, and had three children, and seemed to be finding some of the security his life had been without for so long.

'I growed up and got married, was tryin' to settle down/The next thing I knew, woman tryin' to put me down.' It was all too young, too uncertain to last. From this first clutch at security his life began to wind down around him. The girl he'd married left him with the children, and to keep everything going he started the endless moving that keeps him going from city to city to find work. He's become a kind of 'regular' on the trip between Oakland and Houston, taking the Greyhound bus from one to the other as jobs open up for him, then run out.

His stomach went within a few years, and in 1963 he lost nearly half of it in an ulcer operation. He was thirty-one, and despite some early recordings for small companies in California and Louisiana, still was going nowhere with his career as a bluesman.

How do you break out of the circle of obscurity that hems you into the small clubs in the ghettos, if you're a young bluesman? If you can't quit — if the blues keeps after you, rising around you when you start to think of your life, your music — then you just go on playing, hoping that something will come along. In 1968, when he was thirty-five, Juke Boy finally got his start. Chris Strachwitz, of Arhoolie Records in Berkeley, put out an lp, and followed it with a second a year later. With the lp's Juke Boy began the long period of working and singing that it takes to get more than a local reputation. It's still hard — there are long stretches without work, despite successful appearances everywhere in the United States and in Europe, and he spends long days of his life riding the Greyhound — but it is beginning for him.

It's difficult to be very poetic about the world that most of the people have to live in, in the cities of the United States or Europe. Even if there's money, clothes, a house — it still is difficult to find a poetic language to deal with it. It could be this is one of the reasons poetry has so small a voice in the society. It's a life lived with things — objects — it's a life lived acquiring the things; and what kind of words can make poetry out of automobile fumes, plastic furniture and frozen food? It is something that the bluesmen try to do, find words to fit around the objects, despite their ugliness.

It can be done — poems can be made out of it. As T.S. Eliot said it isn't the things themselves but the intensity of the poet's response to the things — so we can feel the rough edge of the reality pressing in on us, like a protruding nail pushing through a shirt sleeve as we lean against a table. And one of the most persistent of the bluesmen doing it is Juke Boy Bonner. Part of what he does is the kind of immediate expression he picked up from Lightnin' Hopkins — a blues out of the day's newspaper — part of it, as well, is his own expression of the kind of personal news that never gets on the pages of a newspaper, but still makes up the sum of a life.

It's in this aspect of his music that he goes back to the old role of the griot, the commentor, the man standing aside to watch what is happening, and to sing about it. It's this that's his legacy as a bluesman, that gives what he does its own shape and dimension. He finds it in the larger songs about the life and struggles of the people around him in Houston, and he finds it as much in his own family. A blues he recorded for Chris Strachwitz, 'I'm In The Big City', is certainly a kind of personal praise song that a village griot might be expected to produce.

My sister and my brother-in-law come a mighty long way,
From sharecropping in 1947, boy, every year they got to find a new place to stay.
Now they got their own place and land for their cattle to graze.

He does many of the ordinary love songs that are the main current of the blues — his songs like 'Real Good Woman' or 'If You Don't Want To Get Mistreated' — or the blues' other subject, lonely wandering, like 'Lonesome Ride Back Home'.

There's gonna be a long, long lonesome ride back home.
There's gonna be a long, long lonesome ride back home.
What hurts me so bad, ain't nobody missed me since I been gone.

Can't get no letter, telephone don't never ring,
Can't get no letter, telephone don't never ring.
It's gonna be a long lonesome ride back home, goin' back home again.

But there is the other side of what he does — the blues that concern themselves with the cities, with the places he had to live. 'Struggle Here in Houston', 'Stay Off Lyons Avenue', 'Houston, The Action Town', from his earlier recordings, and the wonderful blues called 'Funny Money' that he did on the economic policy brought in by President Nixon late in his first term — the price and salary freeze.

Doctor take me off penicillin because it give me a rash,

Now the president took me off cash,
  All the money got funny,
  Man, my money got funny,
I ain't jivin' you baby, sure make my money get funny.

I couldn't get the raise I been waitin' on so long,
Nixon told me the freeze was on,
  Yeah, money got funny,
  Money got real funny,
I ain't jivin', man my money gets real funny.

This definition of himself as a bluesman didn't always have this other aspect. Juke Boy did two early groups of recordings, before his first album on Arhoolie. His first session was with a small company in Oakland run by Bob Geddings, an Oakland man who tried singles with most of the artists who came in and out of the Bay area. In 1957 Juke Boy did 'Well Baby' and 'Rock With Me Baby', for Geddings' Irma label. They were ordinary blues, released under the name 'Juke Boy Barner', and he had a second guitarist, Lafayette Thomas, working with him. His next sessions, as Juke Boy Bonner, 'The One Man Trio' — because he played the guitar, played the harmonica, and sang — were for Eddie Schuler, who ran a number of small labels from Lake Charles, Louisiana, and they were like the first blues he did. Everything came out from the session, most of it on a European lp, and the titles were familiar phrases like 'Let's Boogie', and 'Going Crazy Over You'. The two sides released to the local market on Schuler's Gold Band label were 'Call Me Juke Boy' and 'Can't Hardly Keep From Crying'.

But unlike most bluesmen his way of writing and singing changed when his career was still taking shape. During the time that he was convalescing from his stomach operation he worked with his blues writing until he had developed it into poems that were free of the restrictions of the blues form — that could be printed without any reference to a melody. He made himself into a poet, in the literary sense of the word. He began to publish regularly in Houston's black newspaper, and he went on writing the poems after he was able to start singing again.

The blues, now, have this other sense in their phrasing, in their language and concerns. It is a larger sense that was always implicit — despite the ornaments hung around the neck of the blues this is the body that was underneath all the decoration. The blues as comment, the blues as a language of criticism and concern.

What's all this gotten Juke Boy? Not much, so far. If you want to listen to him play and you don't happen to be near a festival or a concert when he's making an appearance, you have to look around the black clubs for him. In some towns the blues still is a neighborhood music — just as years after the great bands of New Orleans had broken up you could still hear music in little dance halls over the city. This is where Juke Boy's liable to be. He still has to keep his household going, though the children are almost old enough to be on their own.

In a small club, sometimes with a drummer, usually by himself, working behind his guitar and his harmonica rack, a nervous, thin man, dressed in casual clothes — you'll find Juke Boy. He does the songs as they come to him, working over personal versions of the newest hit records if the songs interest him. He's loose and irregular about the chord changes and the phrase lengths — as Lightnin' Hopkins is — but the rhythm's always there. If it's a medium shuffle it stays a medium shuffle. People can get up and dance to it — and in the clubs he works people usually do. Sometimes he gets a job in one of the folk clubs in a university town, and he doesn't have to think about dancing or the records on the juke box behind him — but the music still has the flow of rhythm, the studied involvement with the words that are part of his blues.

The role of the entertainer in other societies — as

historian or poet or commentor — is something that Juke Boy would recognize, even if the style of the music or its context was different. It's this larger role that we recognize in him, the bluesman who is the historian of his society, as well as its entertainer. And it's this that keeps him going, from town to town, from job to job, his nervous face staring sadly out of the window of a Greyhound Bus.

THE LANGUAGE , THE VOICE

In Louisiana

THE LANGUAGE, THE VOICE

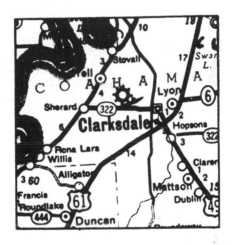

The modern blues, like any form of popular music, has become multi-dimensioned, and it has functions within the black society that extend from entertainment — the blues played as dance music in a neighborhood bar — to the blues as an intensely personal self-expression. Any of these functions is a key to understanding the blues, but one of the most significant aspects of the blues that has to be understood is the language of the blues itself. It is a distinct language — a speech — that grew out of the isolation, the poverty, and the racism that have hemmed in the black American since the first slaves were landed in the colonies in the early 1600's.

It would seem obvious that this language — 'dialect' as it's more strictly defined — would be at the root of the black expression in America, but it was forced to remain in a half-world of imitation or suppression, until it became another badge of the black society's otherness. What is the first expression we have of the black experience in America? It isn't — as someone would expect — a kind of pre-blues language; instead it was the assimilated language of the white culture. In the early years the only black voices that could be heard were voices that had forced themselves to sound white. One of the first pieces to be published by a slave was this poem by Phillis Wheatley.

Celestial choir! enthron'd in realms of light,
Columbia's scenes of glorious toils I write.
While freedom's cause her anxious breast alarms,
She flashes dreadful in refulgent arms.
See mother earth her offspring's fate bemoan,
And nations gaze at scenes before unknown!
See the bright beams of heaven's revolving light
Involved in sorrows and the veil of night! . . .

The poem was a tribute to George Washington, a slaveholder, written by a slave, and it still could talk about 'freedom's cause', which was the kind of irony that assimilation forced on to someone who tried it. The poem ends,

Proceed, great chief, with virtue on thy side,
Thy ev'ry action let the goddess guide.
A crown, a mansion, and a throne that shine,
With gold unfading, Washington! be thine.

'Phillis' — the name given her by her owner — was captured in Senegal when she was about eight years old and brought to Boston in 1761. A successful tailor, John Wheatley, bought her to be trained as a personal servant for his wife. With the help of Wheatley's wife and daughter she learned to read and write, and by the time she was seventeen she published her first poem, 'A Poem by Phillis, A Negro Girl in Boston, on the Death of the Revered George Whitefield'. Three years later she became sick and the doctors recommended a sea voyage. Wheatley's wife freed her and sent her to London where she was an immediate social success as the 'Negro poetess'. Her poems were collected there and published in 1773, *Poems on Various Subjects, Religious and Moral.*

For the scattered slaves being raised as house servants in the northern colonies there was little chance for anything except a kind of cultural assimilation, and the owners often were pleased that their slaves could do something as complicated as read and write, a skill not common among the poorer white colonists. The Bible was usually the book used as a teaching source — and it also reinforced the determination of the owner to turn the slaves into Christians. This obliterated the African culture that had shaped every aspect of the African life, but the people concerned with both slaves and 'free' men accepted it as a sign that they were justified in what they were doing — since their slaves were now Christian and 'educated'.

In the larger plantations, where the slaves were herded into large groups as field workers, a distinct slave culture was beginning to take shape. But there is almost no trace of its first tentative beginnings. The small thread of black expression that did emerge had lost its blackness. Even before Phillis Wheatley a slave in the western Massachusetts village of Deerfield, Lucy Terry, had written about the Indian attack on the settlement in 1746, and her poem is like other doggerel ballads of the period.

> *August 'twas the twenty fifth*
> *Seventeen hundred forty-six*
> *The Indians did in ambush lay*
> *Some very valiant men to slay*
> *The names of whom I'll not leave out*
> *Samuel Allen like a hero fout*

And though he was so brave and bold
His face no more shall we behold.
Eleazer Hawks was killed outright
Before he had time to fight
Before he did the Indians see
Was shot and killed immediately.
Oliver Amsden he was slain
Which caused his friends much grief and pain . . .

Of the African cultures, with their great traditions of chanted poetry and professional song historians, little survived. If there were epic poems chanted in secret meetings in the forests, they were lost — since they couldn't even have been understood by the slave owners, and their African language was unwritten. The first published work by a slave was a prayer, Jupiter Hammon's 'An Evening Thought: Salvation by Christ, with Penitential Cries', that appeared as a printed broadside in 1760. It is an assembly of Christian commonplaces, despite occasional lines with references to 'dark benighted Souls', or 'set the Sinner free', phrases that occur as freely in white devotional verse of the same period.

Salvation comes by Christ alone,
The only Son of God;
Redemption now to every one,
That love his holy Word,
Dear Jesus we would fly to Thee,
And leave off every Sin . . .

The voices were dulled, forced, constrained. Language and expression come from the thrust of experience — the rhythms cluster around the rhythms of the excitements, the emotions of the life. This was language learned by memorization and example, the way any immigrant begins to learn. It wasn't their own language, but something they'd been forced to put on, like the swathes of clothes that had been hung around the women's shoulders. When a slave in North Carolina, George Horton, was permitted to write about his emotions as a slave it had to be forced through the language of the people who had enslaved him.

Alas! and am I born for this,
* To wear this slavish chain?*
Deprived of all created bliss,
* Through hardship, toil and pain!*

How long have I in bondage lain,
* And anguished to be free!*
Alas! and must I still complain —
* Deprived of liberty . . .*

Horton's story has a baffled desperateness to it as he tried to find some way to get free — through the illusory opening he thought he saw in assimilation. He was at Chapel Hill from his birth in 1797, much of the time working outside his owners' house as a servant to the President of the university. He managed to learn to read and write, and he began to write for the students, composing their love poems for twenty or twenty-five cents. Finally in 1829 he managed to have a book of his original poems published, *The Hope Of Freedom*. The hope was that he'd get enough money from the book to buy his freedom. The book didn't get him the money, and he was forced to remain a slave, writing his bitter protests at what was happening to his life. When freedom did finally come it was only through violence and force. The Union armies fought their way into North Carolina in 1865, and despite his age — 68 by this time — and the dreary myth that the old slaves wept at being forced to leave their masters — he managed to escape and make his way to the Federal lines. He went on to Philadelphia, and almost as an act of defiance lived on for another eighteen years.

There were efforts to collect early examples of slave dialects, but they were begun in the 19th Century, after nearly two hundred years of contact between the two groups. However, the Gullah language of the Georgia Sea Islands had been held almost in a state of suspension because of the isolation of the islands, and a Southerner,

Charles C. Jones, Jr., collected many of the stories from the islands and published them in the 1880's. The linguist William A. Stewart has quoted one of the tales as Jones transcribed it.

Buh Lion bin a hunt, and eh spy Buh Goat leddown topper er big rock wuk eh mout an der chaw. Eh creep up fuh ketch um. Wen eh git close ter um eh notus um good. Buh Goat keep on chaw. Buh Lion try fuh fine out wuh Buh Goat duh eat. . .

In Stewart's English version this is,

Brother Lion was hunting and he spotted Brother Goat lying down on a big rock, chewing with his mouth. He crept up to catch him. When he got close to him he looked him over carefully. Brother Goat kept on chewing. Brother Lion tried to find out what Brother Goat was eating . . .

This early language is similar, in many aspects, to the modern 'pidgin', the dialect spoken in sections of West Africa colonized by the English. It is clearly different from the acquired English of George Horton or Phillis Wheatley, and it is also closer to the tonal sound and speech rhythm of the blues dialect.

But the force of the separate black expression began to emerge in the mid-19th Century, through the spiritual. Even in the diluted and sentimentalized form that the spiritual filtered through to the white society, it was obvious that it was a uniquely different musical and textual form, even if much of the imagery was derivative. What the spiritual was — when it first emerged from the cross-fertilization of the permitted Christian ritual and the suppressed African social expression and tribal belief — is probably impossible to trace. But the spirit of it is still continuing in the small store front churches in every American city with a ghetto population. The song chant, here, under the dangling glare of the lights on the worn wood of seats and unpainted benches, is still a freely poeticized response to the raw reality of the day's experience — expressed in a complex metaphor of Christian belief.

But the spiritual was a voice — and not of assimilation. It is more direct, it is closer to the black language. As noted by casual travelers the shape of the language was becoming clearer.

Ezekiel saw that wheel
Way up in the middle of the air.
Ezekial saw that wheel
Way up in the middle of the air.

And the big wheel run by faith
And the little wheel run by the Grace of God
A wheel within a wheel
Way in the middle of the air.

I wonder where my mudder gone;
Sing, O graveyard!
Graveyard ought to know me;
Ring Jerusalem!

Grass grow in de graveyard;
Sing, O graveyard!
Graveyard ought to know me;
Ring, Jerusalem!...

De foxes hab holes,
An' de birdies hab nes',
But de Son ob Man he hab not where
To lay de weary head.

(Chorus)

Jehovyah, Hallelujah! De Lord He will purvide!
Jehovyah, Hallelujah! De Lord He will purvide!...

Mary and Marthy had a chair —
Walk Jerus'lem jis like Job!
An' a eb'ry link was a Jesus Name
Walk Jerus'lem jis like Job!

When I comes ter die I want ter be ready;
When I comes ter die
Gwine ter walk Jerus'lem jis like Job!

81

I tell you, bredderin, fur a fac' —
Walk Jerus'lem jis like Job!
If you ebber leabs de debbil you mustn't turn back!
Walk Jerus'lem jis like Job!

> *When I comes ter die I want ter be ready;*
> *When I comes ter die*
> *Gwine ter walk Jerus'lem jis like Job! .·. .*

Ride on, Jesus, Ride on, Jesus,
Ride on conqu'ring king;
> *I want to go to Heaven in de mornin'.*

See my mudder, Oh, yes, Tell her for me, Oh, yes,
Ride my hoss in de battle ob de field,
> *I want to go to Heaven in de mornin' . . .*

How much of the language of the spirituals is a suppressed communication dealing with the immediate problems of slave life, and how much is simple repetition of the clichés of white religion? This has been violently argued for years, and there would seem to be no satisfactory resolution of the problem. One book has claimed that virtually all the spirituals are directly significant as a slave expression — even claiming that some of the best known were composed by active black revolutionary leaders. This is difficult to make credible, since virtually the same language and text exist in the body of white hymnology that the black inherited. 'You got to cross that river' can refer directly to a landmark or an obstacle in the flight out of the South — it can mean a specific southern river — or it can mean, simply, the familiar River of Jordan.

But a verse like this, collected in the South in the nineteenth century, is more difficult to classify.

Who dat yonder dressed in white?
Must be de chillun ob de Ismelite.
> *Done found dat new hidin' place!*

Who dat yonder dressed in red?
Must be de chillun dat a Moses led!
> *Done found dat new hidin' place!*

Come along —
    Done found dat new hidin' place!
I'se so glad I'm
    Done found dat new hidin' place!

It could mean the familiar hiding place in the bosom of the Lord — or it could be an indirect reference to a hiding place on a runaway route. The ex-slave Frederick Douglass, who escaped from Baltimore in the 1830's and later wrote a classic account of his life, *My Life In Bondage*, said that for him and for other slaves the spirituals had a direct, close immediacy. They interpreted the words in terms of their own desperate situation, and the pain and the unhappiness they sang about was their own.

A complicating aspect in the spiritual — for researchers examining the textual material later — is the identification of the slave with the Hebrew children — 'de chillun ob de Ismelite'. The Bible and the white hymns are filled with references to the delivery of the children of Israel from their slavery in Egypt. The desperateness with which some of the spirituals cling to this notion has the same forlorn hopelessness of the Ghost Dance ceremonies of the Plains Indians at the end of the Nineteenth Century, when they turned to magic ceremonies to drive out the white man and bring back the buffalo. A women researcher interviewed a black song leader in the late 1890's, and the singer, without realizing it, did point out one of the most dominant themes of the spiritual — that there is a rebirth after death. This was not a continuation of the African cult death tradition of return to the homeland — which led to the suicide of many slaves — but it had become, by this time, the spiritual rebirth of traditional Christianity. The attempt to imitate the flavor of the voice of the speaker was almost more of a difficulty than a help, but it was characteristic of much of the research of the period.

'. . . At home there used to be a rare old singer, an old Kentucky mammy, whom everybody loved. She once said: "Use ole heads use ter make 'em up on de spurn of de moment, arter we wrassle wid de Sperit and come thoo. But the tunes were brung from Africa by our granddaddies. Dey was jus 'miliar songs. Dese days dey calls 'em ballots, but in de old days dey call 'em spirituals, case de Holy Spirit done revealed 'em to 'em. Some say Moss Jeses taught 'em, and I's seed 'em start in meetin'. We'd all be at the prayer house de Lord's Dat, and de white preacher he'd splain de word and read what Ezekial done say —

Dry bones gwine ter lib ergin

And honey, de Lord would come a-shinin' thoo dem pages and revive dis old nigger's heart, and I'd jump up dar and den and and holler and shout and sing and pat, and dey would all cotch de words and I'd sing it to some old shout song I'd heard 'em sing from Africa, and dey'd all take it up and keep at it, and keep a-addin' to it, and den it would be a spiritual. Dese spirituals am de best moanin' music in de world, case dey is de whole Bible sung out and out . . '

And the spirituals do have something else — the inflection and tone of black speech.

But a people's speech — even their religious expression — isn't necessarily the language of their literature, especially when there is another speech superimposed over all of it. The speech is what people say to each other — it's the language they use when they stand on a street corner talking, when a mother talks to a child, when a man and woman make love. And until their literature grows from this daily speech their culture is still crippled and lame. It still is fragmented in the confusions between the two languages — until, almost as in a translation, the rich variety of the original is lost, and the new version — the formal version — is a stiff, uncomfortable version of the new language. For the black community in America the literature was the song, the story, the music that had been forged in the new experience — but its expression was still presented in a stilted version of the alien English.

A black poet, Paul Laurence Dunbar, was successful at the turn of the century with his poems in what was considered a faithful rendering of black speech. The poems did have some of the tonality, but the grammatical forms were rooted in English usage,

G'way an' quit dat noise, Miss Lucy —
Put dat music book away;
What's de use to keep on tryin'?
Ef you practis twell you're gray,
You cain't sta't no notes a-flyin'
Lak de ones dat rants and rings
F'om de kitchen to de big woods
When Malindy sing. . .

and the sentimentality, as well as the poetic forms themselves, were derivative. The poetry was a black version of what sentimental 'local color' writers were doing with white vernacular speech.

It was only in the half-world of the musician that there was a consciousness of the separate language, and words began to cross over. 'Jass' is the obvious example. It was a clouded, uncertain period. Something was happening, but its shape could only dimly be glimpsed through the vague shadow surrounding black society in the United States. It was, finally, in the mid-twenties that the light broke through the clouds — with the first country blues recordings there was finally a clear glimpse of the speech, the voice of black America.

It is true that before the first country blues recordings there had been a period of recording by urban blues artists and by black jazz groups — but the songs were still filtered through the sieve of the white music industry. The texts were generally ridden with the same clichés that had dominated black writing for the musical stage since the days of the minstrel show. It was only with the country bluesmen that the language became authentic — that it had the inflection and the richness of the spoken language. It was the way people talked to each other on the street, the way men and women talked to each other. Of all the things that are the legacy of the blues it's probably this that is the most important — that with the blues the black American, for the first time, was able to speak with his own voice.

It was immediately clear that the blues was a distinctive language, despite the clumsy and often racist marketing practices of the white companies that were responsible for the early recordings — but it was also a voice that many blacks couldn't fully accept, since it was a language so different from the white that it seemed to emphasise their place outside the larger society. But, as linguists have learned, black speech is more than a clumsy effort to ape white speech — it is a language of its own. The linguist William A. Stewart has worked for years with black speech in both Africa and the United States; he has written — in conjunction with Cheikh Babou — an introductory course in the Wolof language of Dakar, and published many articles on the problem of black speech in the white schools, and he has said of the speech of the slaves, in an article called 'Understanding Black Language',

> ... this type of early Afro-American English was structured, from a linguistic point of view. A linguist could write a grammar of it. He could write a dictionary of it. He could also write a description of the sound system because it very early acquired a certain kind of uniformity — so much that when one compares the records of this early slave speech, one finds that it is surprisingly consistent from one person to another. It was in a sense the same language spoken by different people . . .

The essential point is that the language of the black American is not simply bad English — but that it is a separate dialect of English, with its own rules and forms. To dismiss it simply as poor speech, as whites have done for years, is as if an Englishman were to dismiss the Scots' language as simply a bad version of their own speech. The fact that the English did take this attitude for many years is indicative of the importance of

English attitudes in the early slave trade. Although there have been many changes in the speech patterns in the last hundred years Stewart feels that the root language for the black American today is the early dialect that developed in the slave culture. The older dialect has survived almost intact in the Gullah language of the islands off the Georgia coast, and there seem to be clear interrelationships between the older language and to-day's speech. As Stewart says again,

There seem to be very clear relationships between this older Gullah and the present-day Negro dialect. These relationships are so strong that research cur-rently going on all over the country seems to make it clear that in no part of the United States do Negroes and whites speak identically; this is especially true of Negroes of a lower socio-economic class. This is important, because with intense education, these differences may fade away so that educated Negroes and whites may speak in the same ways in many areas. But white and Negro people who haven't been strongly influenced by education — particularly in the stable, traditional towns and rural areas of the United States — still speak in remarkably different ways even though they have lived side by side for centuries. It is this real difference which is the basis for the much misused stereotype of Negro speech.

It is in the language that much of the blues' wiry strength lies. It is not the whole expression of the black society in America, but it is one of the most vital. It would be possible to trace the social struggle in America through the language of the blues singers, as the older dialect forms that were at the heart of the rural blues gave way to the newer forms in the city blues — and as the language forms of the city blues have given way to the pop forms of the soul artists, whose language approaches more and more directly the surrounding white speech.

A country singer like Big Joe Williams still uses the older dialect forms.

When I first left home, tookin' Mississippi delta to be
my home,
When I first left home, tookin' Mississippi delta to be
my home.
My baby gone, hang my head and moan.

I left my dear mother standin' in the doorway cryin'
I left my dear mother standin' in her doorway cryin'
She said, son don't never worry, you got a home be
long just I got mine . . .

(When I First Left Home)

. . . I'm goin' back to Crawford, Mississippi, believe
I'll settle down,
I'm going back to Crawford, Mississippi, believe I'll
settle down,
You got me out here on the delta, rollin' from town
to town.

I'm goin' back to Crawford, believe I'll change my
name,
I'm goin' back to Crawford, I believe I'll change my
name,
I been wrong, woman, but you runnin' 'round with
another man.

(I Been Wrong But I'll Be Right)

All of his songs have the compressed phrasing, the
elimination of unnecessary tense and adverb construction, that are distinctive in the blues language. Even the
so-called grammatical errors, such as double negatives
and incomplete forms, have to be considered basic to
the dialect, since they're used so consistently.

Woman I'm lovin', sleepin' in her grave,
Woman I'm lovin', sleepin' in her grave.
Well, the fool I hate meet her every day.

Please don't give my woman no job,
Please don't give my baby no job,
She's a married woman, and I don't 'low her to work
too hard . . .

(Levee Break Blues)

These same forms occur again and again in all of the blues. Juke Boy Bonner has been singing in the cities for years, but his texts still use the older dialect forms.

They say you can't let your troubles, oh man, get you down,
You can't let your troubles, oh lord, get you down,
But what can you do when you got problems all around.

I know worryin' and cryin', ain't gonna help at all,
Worryin', worryin' and cryin' about it ain't gonna help at all.
Every time my door bell rings, there go another problem comin' to call . . .

(Problems All Around)

The language of the blues is a clear reflection of a dialect forming away from the influence of the white culture. It is so strongly associated with the blues that now it has become difficult to consider one apart from the other. For much of the black community the dialect is almost an anachronism, as they have become more closely associated with the white culture and their own language has ceased to be so strongly rooted in the linguistic patterns that form the blues speech. But the blues, itself, continues to have its distinctive language form. Even a singer who has been out of the rural background for most of his life, like Champion Jack Dupree, still uses the dialect for his blues writing.

I woke up this morning, found my baby gone,
I woke up this morning, found my baby gone.
Well, she wrote me a letter,
        sayin' one day I'll be back home.

She said, 'Darlin', I'm gon' leave you
        on the fifteenth of Máy.'
She said 'Darlin', I'm gon' leave you
        on the fifteenth of May.'
I said, 'Baby, please don't leave me,
        cause you'll be gone to stay . . .'

(Found My Baby Gone)

. . . Nobody helps me and everybody knows I's down
and out,
Nobody helps me and everybody knows I's down and
out
You come along to me, baby, and you really pulled
me out.

You's a real good woman, you helped me when I
couldn't help myself,
Yes, you's a real good woman you helped me I
couldn't, I couldn't help myself.
I don't care where I go around the world I'll never
have nobody else.   (Down And Out)

The difference becomes more clear when this speech is related to the speech forms of an urban artist, whose milieu has been the city ghetto, like Mighty Joe Young.

Oh now it's early in the morning,
         and I need to say a prayer,
I'm about to lose my woman,
         and I'm pullin' out my hair.
It's early in the morning,
   Early in the morning, child,
   Early in the morning,
   Early in the morning, child.

Now, it's early in the morning,
         the store ain't open yet,
I need a little something, you all,
         to get my throat wet.
So early in the morning,
   Yes, in the wee wee hours,
   So early in the morning,
   Early in the morning, child . . .

But it is a speech, it is a language, and it is in language that self definition begins, and beyond that it is in the definition of self that the self begins to come together out of the fragments of experience. In the language of the blues was a legacy of black speech that was a first expression of the human being who was the black American.

90

THE BLUES AS POEM

Johnny Wrencher and John Lee Grandison, Maxwell Street, Chicago

THE BLUES AS POEM

Days of Old

Well, it's back in the time when peoples was considered
was a slave, you know they was workin' from what I say
can to can't, they couldn't see when they come in, couldn't
see hardly when they go out and you know they wasn't
gettin' no pay, and they was gettin' what the man give
'em — that's what I consider of slaves.

Oh, I been workin' on the levee, lord, captain, I been
   sleepin' on the ground.

Uumh — lord, man, I was sleepin' on the ground.
If that don't kill a good man, lord, lord,
    it sure get you down.

Anybody ask me, oh lord, how come I'd of leave,
Ooh, anybody ever ask me, oh lord, how come I had to leave.
You can tell them I got tired of them old rice and salmon,
    oh lord, and them black-eyed peas.

If I be late Monday morning tell the man to don't 'pend on me.
Oh lord, if I be late Monday morning tell the man, oh lord,
    don't 'pend on poor me.
I'm gon' catch that old mornin' local, boy, oh lord, and
    make my get a way.

Uumh, something up the line keep on worryin' me.
Uumh, something up the road worries me.
That little old girl of mine, call her Ida Mae.

Sunnyland Slim

Couldn't Find A Mule

Lord, I worked old Maude this morning, God knows
    I done worked old Belle
Oh, I worked old Maude, captain, you know I done
    worked old Belle
I couldn't find a mule in that whole corral, lord,
    that had its shoulder well.

I been kind of worried, I been thinkin' 'bout
    what's been goin' on
You know I been kind of worried, lord, I been had
    my travelin' shoes on
I seed the captain whip the water boy, and durn
    near bust his head.

Uumh, oh lord, oh lord, oh lord, (sp. gets prayers
    in it)

94

Oh lord, oh lord, oh lord, oh lord,
An' I thought about what my mother and father said,
  it's never too late to pray.

You know I told the captain that my mother was dead
Oh, I told the bossman early this morning, lord,
  that my poor mother was dead.
He said, Negro, if you don't go to work, you soon
  will be dead too.

(sp. Here's what I said)
Uumh, lord have mercy on my poor sinkin' soul
Uumh — have mercy on a poor man's sinkin' soul
The devil's got the badge of that white man, it's
  too late for him to try to pray.

Sunnyland Slim

Lone Wolf

I'm that wolf that's howlin', woman, that me
  howlin' 'round your door.
I'm that lone wolf that's howlin', woman, that me
  howlin' 'round your door.
If you just give me what I want, little girl, won't
  help me when I howl no more.

Well, you get up in the morning, I'll be howlin'
  'round your door
Yeh, you get up in the morning, I'll be howlin'
  'round your door
If you give me what I want, little woman, you won't
  have any call when I howl no more.

I want a girl forgive a black man most anything I do,
Yeh, I wonder do my baby forgive me any old thing I do
Well, I'm dark complexioned, wonder will you forgive
  me too.

You gonna get up in the morning, howlin' 'round your
   door
Well, early in the morning I be howlin' 'round your door
If you give me what I want you won't help me when
   I howl no more.

Big Joe Williams

Levee Break Blues

Woman I'm lovin' sleepin' in her grave
Woman I'm lovin' sleepin' in her grave
Well, the fool I hate, meet her every day.

Please, don't give my woman no job
Please, don't give my baby no job
She's a married woman, and I don't 'low
   her to work too hard.

Oh, early in the morning 'bout the break
   of day
Early in the morning, baby, about the break
   of day
I'm goin' to grab the pillow where my baby
   used to lay.

Take me out of the bottom before the water rise
Take me out of the bottom, baby, before the
   water rise
Don't want to be buried down on the levee side.

Big Joe Williams

Black Gal, You're Sure Lookin' Warm

Black gal, sure lookin' warm,

Black gal, sure lookin' warm,
You done cause me to break up my happy home.

Black gal, sure lookin' good,
Oh, black gal, you sure lookin' good,
Well, you got any place, darlin' I sure could.

Black gal, you sure lookin' warm,
Black gal, you sure lookin' warm,
You done got to the place you can break
    my happy home.

Don't you wish your black gal was little and
    low like mine
Oh, don't you wish your black gal was little and
    low like mine
Everytime she walks she make my love fall down.

Black gal, sure lookin' warm,
Oh, black gal, you sure lookin' warm,
You drive any man 'way from his happy home.

                                    Big Joe Williams

I Been Wrong But I'll Be Right

I been wrong, but I'll be right someday
I been wrong, people, but I'll be right someday
Well, I know you goin' be sorry you treated me
    this a way.

I'm goin' back to Crawford, Mississippi, believe
    I'll settle down,
I'm goin' back to Crawford, Mississippi, I believe
    I'll settle down.
Well, you got me out here on the delta, rollin'
    from town to town.

I'm goin' back to Crawford, believe I'll change
    my name,
I'm goin' back to Crawford, I believe I'll change
    my name
I been wrong, woman, but you runnin' 'round with
    another man.

I ain't got nobody no to give my money to
I ain't got nobody no give my money to
I been wrong, woman, the way I been treatin' you.

Big Joe Williams

Slidin' Delta

Oh, Slidin' Delta done been here and gone,
    Here me cryin' — I ain't got —
Oh, Slidin' Delta done been here and gone.
It make me think about my baby, ooah, ooah, ooah.

Oh, early this mornin', creepin' through my door,
    Now don't you a-hear me cryin', pretty mama,
Early this mornin', cryin' through my door.
Well, I hear that whistle blow and she won't blow
    here no mo'.

Oh, slow down train now, bring my baby back home,
    Now don't you a-hear me cryin', pretty mama,
Slow down train, bring my baby back home.
Well, she been gone so long, ooah, make my poor
    heart burn.

One thing now I don't understand,
    Now don't you a-hear me cryin', pretty mama,
One thing now I don't understand.
I been nice to my baby, ooah, she gone with
        another man.

Oh, thought I heard freight train whistle blow,
  Now don't you a-hear me cryin', pretty mama,
Thought I heard freight train whistle blow,
And she blowed just like, ooah, ooah, ooah.

Oh, run here, mama, sit down on my knee,
  Now don't you hear me cryin', pretty mama,
Run here, mama, sit down on my knee.
I want to understand now, baby, ooh, how you
  treat poor me.

Oh, two trains runnin' now, runnin' side by side,
  Now don't you hear me cryin', pretty mamma
Two trains runnin' now, runnin' side by side.
Well, these one of the trains, ooah, ooah, ooah.

Now come on home, baby, come to me,
  You know I'm lovingest man can be,
Oh, come on home, come on home to me.
You know I need your love, baby, just as a man can be.

          J.D. Short

Rare Dog Blues

Oh, early this mornin' I heard my rare dog bark,
Oh, early this mornin' I heard my rare dog bark,
Well, my love has gone away, she trippin' somewhere.
Well, 'count your whinin', know my baby lay around,
Well, 'count of your whinin' know my baby near
  run off,
You can't hide from em baby, 'cause I ain't gonna let
  you put me down.

Come home soon in the morning, 'cause you stayed
  away all last night
Come home soon in the morning, you stayed away all
  last night

I want to know from you, baby, do you call that
    treatin' me right.

Well, the wee wee hours, no one keep my company
Well, in the wee wee hours, no one to keep my
    company
Well, I got blues 'bout my baby, I'm blue as any
    man can be . . .

J.D. Short

I'm A Bluesman

My father passed on when I was two years old,
Didn't leave me a thing but a whole lot of soul.
    You can see I'm a bluesman,
    Man, man, you know I'm a bluesman.
I want the whole world to know why I'm a bluesman.

My mother passed on when I was just about eight,
I started to learn I was growin' up in a world of
    hate.
    That made me a bluesman,
    You can see why I'm a bluesman.
I want the whole world to understand what made me
    into a bluesman.

I go to work in the fields when I was just thirteen,
Didn't get a chance to know what education means.
    I'm a bluesman,
    Man, that made me a bluesman.
I want the whole world to know what it takes to make
    a real bluesman.

I growed up and got married, was tryin' to settle down,
The next thing I knew woman tryin' to put me down.
    That made me a bluesman,

Man, that made me a bluesman.
Man, tellin' you the truth what it takes to make a
    real bluesman.

Lay down at night you don't know where you're goin'
    to sleep,
Where on earth your next meal to eat,
        That make you a bluesman,
        Uumh, bluesman.
I want the whole world to know how come I'm a bluesman.

                                    Juke Boy Bonner

Funny Money

Doctor take me off penicillin because it give me a rash,
Now the president took me off of cash,
        All the money got funny,
        Man, my money got funny.
I ain't jivin' you baby,
        Sure made my money get funny.

I couldn't get the raise I been waitin' on so long,
Nixon told me the freeze was on.
        Yeah, money got funny,
        Money got real funny.
I ain't jivin', man,
        My money gets real funny.

Preacher took me off of sinnin' because he says
    it's savin' my soul,
Now the government takes my woman off the welfare roll.
        Boy, that *is* funny,
        Man, that make the money get real funny.
Man I ain't jivin', man,
        Money got real funny.

Funny, funny money,
    But I mean real funny, brothers, real funny.

                                        Juke Boy Bonner

Problems All Around

They say you can't let your troubles, oh man, get you down.
You can't let your troubles, oh lord, get you down.
But what can you do, when you got problems all around.

I know worryin' and cryin', ain't gonna help at all,
Worryin, worryin' and cryin' about it ain't gonna help
    at all.
Every time my doorbell rings, there go another problem
    comin' to call.

Babe, I got my problems, babe, I got problems all around.
Look like I got my problems, baby, got my problems all arour
I can't get ahead, baby, for bein' held down.

                                        Juke Boy Bonner

Tired Of The Greyhound Bus

I'm gettin' tired ridin' that old Greyhound,
I'm gettin' tired, ridin' that old Greyhound,
I ain't no worry 'bout the service,
        but they just keep on layin' my bags
        around.

Well, I went to Chicago to pay my debts, went there
    to play the gig,
Chicago, to pay my debts, and I went there to play my gig.
When I got to the station,

I didn't have nothin' to play it with.

I didn't have my guitar, and man can you understand,
Didn't have no guitar, man can you understand,
'Less I play my guitar don't no money in my hand.

So I'm gettin' tired, I don't want to raise no fuss,
But I'm gettin' tired, I don't want to raise no fuss,
But I'm gettin' tired of messin' with them people
 down there,
    that drive those Greyhound busses.

Ummh, uumh
I'm gettin' tired of messin' around,
    ridin' that Greyhound bus.
Well I can't get my luggage on time,
   I got a reason to raise a fuss.

           Juke Boy Bonner

Will It Be

Oh Lord, how long it'll be how long will it be,
Oh Lord, will it be,
   When the time, when the time, comes for me.

Will it be there, will it be hard, will it be misery,
   or will it be pain,
Oh Lord, how long it'll be,
Oh Lord, how long will it be?

I have suffered all my life,
   and I been misery, heart ache, and pain,
I been everything in the world,
   I been every, everything but a human being,
There is no more, no more sorrow,
And no more tears and pain,

Oh Lord, don't let me be,
Oh Lord, be in no pain.

(sp.)   How long could it be,
      No one could tell to be in misery,

      We all have a debt to pay
      When it come you pay.
      That mean somebody, somebody's got to go,
      But it's no use cryin',
      Cryin' don't help you none,
      Just go on like every other person does
      Just ask the good lord above
      To forgive you of your sins
          And take care of you.

God will take care of you,
      No matter what you do.
I know, yes I know,
      He will, he will, he will take care of you.
May the good Lord in heaven, hope he will remember me,
Will it be, will it be,
Oh Lord, will it be?

Champion Jack Dupree

Roamin' Special

Lord, I'm a weak man, some say I got a very weak heart,
Yes, I'm a weak man, some say I got a very weak heart,
But when it comes, comes down to lovin' I can always
    make a start.

Lord, the woman that I love she takes my appetite.
Lord, the woman I'm lovin' she takes my appetite.
She's the sweetest woman I ever seen in my life.

She's got a face like a monkey, she's got hair like a
    teddy bear,

She's got a face like a monkey, she got hair like a
    teddy bear,
She's the ugliest woman that I ever seen anywhere.

She's got pretty smooth skin, just like a
    elephant's hide.
She's got pretty smooth skin, just like a
    elephant's hide.
When you see that ugly woman, partner, you'll know
    that I ain't lyin'.

She's got great big legs 'bout the size of Georgia hams
She got great big legs 'bout the size of Georgia hams
When that woman starts to lovin', she'll sure get you
    in a jam.

Champion Jack Dupree

Vietnam Blues

Lord, I feel so sorry
    for the people over in Vietnam.
Yes, I feel so sorry
    for the people over in Vietnam.
It's a whole lot of things
    Uncle Sam don't understand.

Why don't they leave Vietnam,
    leave those poor people alone.
Won't they leave Vietnam,
    leave those poor people alone.
They got a hell of a problem,
    just like I have at home.

Well, I know every mother
    be glad to see her sons come home.
Yes, I know every mother,

105

be glad to see her sons come home.
Yes, Uncle Sam just as well pack up,
    pull out and go back home.

Lord, the war in Vietnam,
    there's one war won't ever end.
Lord, the war in Vietnam,
    there's one war won't ever end.
Lord, the Vietnam people,
    they got a whole lot of friends.

When the lights come on
    all over the world again.
Yes, when the lights come on
    all over the world again.
Well, the people in Vietnam
    will have a whole lot of friends again.

Champion Jack Dupree

Found My Baby Gone

I woke up this morning, found my baby gone.
I woke up this morning, found my baby gone.
Well, she wrote me a letter,
    sayin' one day I'll be back home.

She said, 'Darlin', I'm gon' leave you
    on the fifteenth of May.'
She said, 'Darlin', I'm gon' leave you
    on the fifteenth of May.'
I said, 'Baby, please don't leave me,
    'cause you'll be gone to stay.'

She say, 'I'll be gone for two years,
    for two years and one day.'
Say, 'I'll be gone for two years,

106

for two years and one day.'
I say, 'I'll hope baby, to see
    your smiling face one day.'

When she caught the plane, I was watchin' it
    go right through the sky.
When she caught the plane, I was watchin' it
    go right through the sky.
Well, it hurt me so bad,
    feel like I want to die.

Lord, I got two women that I can't tell apart.
Lord, I got two women that I can't tell apart.
One is my living,
    and the other one's my heart.

Champion Jack Dupree

Snooks Eaglin

Snooks Eaglin

FINGERS THAT MOVE
- Snooks Eaglin

It could be said, since essentially it's true, that there is no blues singer named Snooks Eaglin. There is a New Orleans guitarist and entertainer who sometimes sings in places like the Playboy Club, doing requests, and his name is Snooks Eaglin. If someone wants to call him a blues singer it doesn't completely get in the way — since he does sing blues — but he never thinks of himself as a bluesman, and the term doesn't really clarify his situation. In the old country term he'd be called a songster, but he isn't old and New Orleans isn't the country. He's a club entertainer, who without consciously considering what he was doing has also become one of the most brilliant of the young blues performers — and that's about as close as it's possible to come to a definition.

But it's also true that there is no more romantic figure in popular music than the bluesman, with everything the term involves. And it isn't a false romanticism, despite the misplaced sentimentality that hangs over it when the response to the music gets too emotional. The bluesman *is* something unique. To call Snooks a blues singer is over-romanticizing him, but it's what we want him to be — and until he clearly turns himself into something else we'll continue to insist that he is. And Snooks will go on recording straight versions of old popular songs like 'I Get The Blues When It Rains', or 1950's rock classics like 'Tomorrow Night', and the confusion will only get deeper.

It isn't only Snooks' voice and singing that begins the confusion. He does have a great blues voice — warm and rough and expressive — but even more than that it's his guitar playing — it's his fingers on the strings and what he can do with them. One of the first things he recorded was an instrumental solo, 'High Society', and it set a kind of standard for acoustical guitar finger picking. Everything else he's recorded has been just as brilliantly played, even when it was a simple chord accompaniment to one of the rock songs. He's one of the most exciting musicians playing the guitar in a style he's made particularly his own.

Probably the most distinctive thing about his style is his looseness. He's one of the most relaxed guitarists in the blues. There's none of the tenseness of the heavy electric blues sound, and there's none of the stiffness of the labored finger picking that's come after both Snooks and Gary Davis. He just swings, with a kind of easy rocking beat that's as casual as a man throwing stones in a summer creek. And along with this looseness he can

112

do everything, any kind of rhythm figure, any kind of sudden solo, whatever he's heard on a record or the radio. His 'High Society' did everything that you'd expect in a full band version — including the solo chorus for clarinet. For the first album after ten years of silence he did 'Pine Top's Boogie Woogie', and it is an eerie imitation of the old piano original. He's recently asked people to send him old 78s by the Jimmy Lunceford Orchestra, so some future session will probably include a version of one of the Lunceford pieces, the arrangement for fifteen instruments transformed into an impeccable, swinging guitar solo.

The whole world of blues guitar is, to a great extent, a white concept. The blues musicians themselves listen to each other's playing, and they do 'rate' each other, but it isn't so important as their singing, as the words to their blues. Sometimes a successful singer will go through his whole career with the same handful of guitar fills that he started out with. For them the guitar is an accompaniment instrument, something to fill out and augment the voice, but it's the voice that's dominant. But for a young white, whatever he tries to feel about the experience of black life in America, the words don't really mean that much. The verses of the blues have only an oblique emotional thrust for him, since the force of most of it is deflected by the difference in the two languages, white and black.

But even if the words weren't so central, there was still the grim desire to be part of the romantic aura surrounding the bluesman. With the two forces working directly on each other it was only a question of time until the other voice of the blues — the guitar — became almost the dominant sound of the white blues. In the black community the great bluesmen are the great singers and writers of verses — in the white community it's the guitar soloists. Snooks, because of his guitar playing, as much as anything else, has become one of the legends of the new blues era.

In one of the pieces he did when he began recording again Snooks talks over some chording on the guitar, and he does say a little about what he thinks as a musician.

'You know one night I heard mama and papa talking and they said I want to let this kid boogie.

Well, let me tell you something, baby, he said we got to get a thing goin', this is the modern age, this ain't the old time age. And a young friend of mine come walking in the back door with a set of drums, you know, and he got to feelin' good so he said, "Looky, here, baby, can I come in and lay some of this funk on you," and I say, "Sure, ain't no sweat."

So he walked in the door like this here — (Snooks beats out a complicated, swinging rhythm on the body of the guitar) — Oh, yeah, Now get down to it, baby, he had to change my mind then, you know . . .

'. . . then we come back another hundred miles, you know, cat cays, "Look here, man, we want to boogie children," — but we saw another drummer. Well, he was about fifty years old, you know. All I could hear, you know, all he was doing, like this somethin' here — (Snooks beats out a labored version of Chicago blues drumming) — Well, that wasn't where it was at, so we took that funky drummer along and what did he do — (he goes back into the first rhythm he was playing on the body of the guitar) — Come on funky! Yeah! — Come on guitar!'

It is pretty much where he is as an artist. The recordings he's most concerned with, of all that he's done, were some sessions as a straight pop-blues singer with his own 'combo' for the Imperial label in New Orleans in 1960 and 1961. It was the band he was usually working with — two saxes, piano, bass, and drums, with himself on guitar. He did a lot of recording — twenty-four sides — released as Ford Eaglin, the record company's version of his real name. There was as always the strong blues sound to all of it, but it wasn't blues. The songs were mostly things that had been popular for other artists, and none of the records sold particularly well, but they are the ones that Snooks feels come closest to how he sees, and hears, himself as a singer.

Nearly all of the men who were recorded during the 'fifties and 'sixties as part of the blues revival were old men, since it was the older blues styles that it was important to preserve while they still had some vitality. But Snooks was young, only 21, and this was part of the excitement over him. He seemed to be continuing a tradition of solo blues — still another reason to go on thinking of him as a bluesman. He was important for what he represented. But this was as much a result of circumstances as anything else. His first recordings were released as folk blues, at the moment when folk blues were suddenly becoming popular.

Snooks was born in New Orleans in 1937, on January 21. He was normal as a baby, but when he was nineteen months old it was found that he had a brain tumor. There was an operation, and it saved his life, but he was left blind from it. More as a toy than anything else his father gave him a guitar when he was six, but he began playing the instrument almost by himself. It didn't matter what kind of music it was, Snooks found a way to play it. He listened to the radio, he listened to records — picking up any kind of music that he liked. By the time he was eleven he was good enough to win a talent contest on the New Orleans radio station WNOE. He did one of his instrumentals, '12th Street Rag'.

New Orleans is a poor town, and it has sprawling neighborhoods of shabby one-story wooden houses, most of them painted white, with a few trees in a trampled backyard and a ragged fringe of flowers in the small bit of ground left next to the sidewalk. It's poor, but it's relaxed, and during the tourist season — which seems to go on almost all year — there's a lot of music, a lot of life on the crowded streets of the French Quarter. Snooks began playing music on the streets in the late

1950's — sometimes by himself, but mostly with friends. Percy Randolph sometimes played harmonica and Lucius Bridges played a second guitar. Snooks played tom-toms for variety. At the same time Snooks was working with an r & b band, that was playing mostly popular hits by other artists.

It's really hard to say that Snooks was much looking for a professional career as a musician. He was like a lot of young musicians in New Orleans who play a little for the tourists, and keep their music as a sideline. New Orleans music is weekend music — men who have other jobs and use the music as much for the pleasure of playing as anything else. Snooks was a lot this way. Dr. Harry Oster, who had also found Robert Pete Williams, heard him playing on the streets and recorded him. There was an album on Folkways in 1959, then one on Prestige — and from the same sessions one that was released in Europe on Storyville label. Oster also did some recording with Snooks and his friends Percy Randolph and Lucius Bridges, and this was released on his own Folk Lyric label.

The variety of songs that Snooks did on his various early records was staggering, from instrumentals like the 'High Society' and 'Malaguena', to folk songs, pop songs, early rock songs, and even some blues — well known songs like 'Every Day I Have The Blues'. The Bluesville lp had the most blues on it, but these were songs from the Bluebird-styled artists of the late 1940's. There isn't a lot of blues in New Orleans — he hadn't heard much blues, so he didn't play it. Except that everything he did had a strong blues flavor to it — and there was always that beautifully loose guitar underneath it.

As slight as his career had been it almost completely ended in the early 1960's. He finally got to record with his combo — the Imperial sessions in 1960 and 1961. The singles he did weren't particularly successful; so he simply stopped recording. He was married in 1960 and his wife, Doretha, took over management of his music

116

and his career. She didn't want him to travel, and she didn't see any reason for him to go on being a folk blues artist, which didn't much interest him anyway. It had been Oster's recording — done by a folklorist for a folk label — that had given him his reputation, and he found it hard to shake off.

For the rest of the 1960's Snooks dropped almost completely out of sight, despite countless offers for concerts and appearances. He and Doretha were living in a small town — St. Rose — outside of New Orleans, and he kept his life out of the city. There were occasional jobs — like the Playboy Club — but for the most part he stayed close to home. He did some playing with an old friend, Roy Byrd, known professionally as Professor Longhair, but there was no more recording. There was no more recording for more than ten years.

Snooks is an elusive and difficult man, and he has been as unavailable to interviewers as he has been to record companies. He finally got to Europe in 1973, but characteristically it was only to London for a week-end private party, and he was there because he was playing with Professor Longhair. But he did talk for a few minutes to the London jazz writer Max Jones. Jones met him in a hotel room when he was waiting to go on and perform. Jones asked him about his name, and he said that it wasn't 'Ford', as all the articles on him have said.

'... When I asked why Snooks instead of Ford, he replied that his real name wasn't Ford but what sounded like Ferd. Ah, I said, as in Ferdinand, like Ferd Morton?

"No," he said, "Fird spelled F-i-r-d. Yes, It's unusual. I can't tell you why I was called that, can't go back that far."

So what about Ford? "Oh, well this was a record company, claimed they never heard of the name Fird, so they changed it to Ford. Imperial named me that in '53."

And Snooks?

A laugh and then: "Did you ever hear of the radio programme Baby Snooks? That was a character, always in trouble. Well, that's how I got that name. I was a bad boy, you believe that, used to swing on the kitchen cabinet, all those things. So they called me Snooks."

... He then asked about Jimmy Lunceford records. Had I the old 78s as he wanted to get them all. He could get them on tape, but that was no good. He wanted all those old 78s, like 'Margie', and 'Well, All Right Then', 'Tain't What You Do', 'Cheatin' On Me'.

"Yeah, that's my music, those big bands that swing. That Jay McShann, he had a band. And Duke, I like his music very much. But Lunceford . . . that was a band." '

It was finally a young New Orleanian, Quint Davis, who was promoting concerts in the city in conjunction with George Wein, who got Snooks back onto the stage again. He managed to get him to play on one of his New Orleans Heritage festivals. In 1971 the Swedish record company, Sonet, asked Davis if there was a chance that Snooks would be willing to record again, and in June, 1971, they went into a studio in Metairie, a New Orleans suburb, and Snooks did an album. Despite the years that had passed nothing much had changed about the music. The guitar work was leaner, sparer, but it was more assured than ever. There was the same range of songs, from the 'Pine Top's Boogie Woogie' to pop things like 'Drive It Home' and 'Tomorrow Night'. He was also singing better than ever, and for the first time there seemed to be critics who sensed what his feelings as a performer really were. There was as pleased a response to the old rock songs as there was to the blues.

But this return to music doesn't necessarily mean that Snooks will become part of the blues scene. He's playing more or less regularly with Professor Longhair, and has done a little touring with him, but Roy Byrd's an energetic and exciting performer who tends to dominate any kind of music around him. On tapes of the band together it's almost impossible to follow what Snooks is doing behind the raw power of Byrd's piano playing. Quint Davis is managing them both; and Snooks wants to keep on doing what he's doing, so there will probably be no more appearances of Snooks Eaglin, bluesman, than there ever were — though he may work out of town as a rhythm guitarist to his old friend Roy Byrd.

Snooks, however, seems unconcerned about all of this. He is uniquely what he is, an exciting young singer and guitarist with a strong blues influence. And there is something in the way he plays the guitar — a kind of easy magic in the feeling of his fingers moving on the strings. It's a mood, a drifting sense of time standing still in the spaces between the notes, that's left its own print on the blues still growing and changing around him.

Champion Jack Dupree

Champion Jack Dupree

HANDS LIKE ELBOWS
- Champion Jack Dupree

It's sometimes difficult to remember that despite the involvement with the blues now it was, like almost every aspect of black culture in the United States, limited to its own social milieu. It grew and developed out of sight of the white community, even though its commercial aspects were largely white controlled. Other forms of black expression, jazz, or the black writing of the '20's, were a more obvious blending of cultural elements, and they attracted considerable attention. But the blues artists were not only tied closely to the essence of the black experience, they were also working at the lowest economic level of the black society. If a few whites noticed them they weren't able to respond to what they were doing. Carl Van Vechten's widely known description of a Bessie Smith performance in the 1920's is one of only a meager handful of sketches like it, and she was a successful theatre artist, appearing in a revue show that was similar to the standard vaudeville fare for the period. The rural blues artists were even farther out of sight, in the lost reaches of poor black America. The closest thing we have to a description of a working bluesman in the 'thirties is a portrait of Champion Jack Dupree working in an Indianapolis night club, by a jazz enthusiast, Duncan P. Schiedt, that catches some of the mood of the blues and its audience, and it's also a glimpse of one of the most durable entertainers of the modern blues era.

A small cone of pink light shot from a ceiling spotlight and bravely tried to penetrate the heavy gray cloud of smoke which hung over the room like a blanket. It landed, considerably weakened, upon the slight frame of a man seated at a piano. His hands played on the keys in a regular rhythm, each hand seeming to battle with the other for predominance. His feet, well away from the pedals, beat out the tempo on the floor. His audience, caught up in the spirit of the rough music he played, danced in the semi-darkness surrounding them. There were other sounds, too, a peal of laughter, heavy coughing, the rustle of clothing as silhouettes passed by a chair, a constant clink of glasses and bottles, the dropping of coins, the sputter of a match, and, off in an adjoining room, the flipping of cards being shuffled and the mutter of gambling men. In that room, too, could be heard the pushing, pulsating rhythm, working its way through lath and plaster, making the whole place a giant sounding board for the blues of Jack Dupree.

This was the second floor of the Cotton Club in Indianapolis, operated by the powerful Negro theatrical booker, Sea Ferguson. One of the dozens of Cotton Clubs established in the wake of the great New York night spot, this was one of the largest. It occupied an old four-story building in the near downtown section, and represented the zenith of black-and-tan night life in the Hoosier capital. On the top floor was the high ceilinged Trianon Ballroom, where the band overlooked the throng of dancers from a high balcony. The Trianon had seen the best of the nation's jazz bands in its day, but just now, in the year 1939, all attention was on the revue type of presentation which held forth on the lower level where several bars and busy waitresses kept the cash registers working steadily.

Dupree's voice now began to make itself heard. He shouted a line of age-old blues, and customers from the circle of tables called out appreciatively. Some of the background noise died down, and people listened for the punch line of his verse, which more often than not struck home in the lusty audience. For many, it was an intimate exchange between themselves and the singer. He seemed to know all about the troubles of the heart, the body or the pocketbook . . .

Jack Dupree was thirty when Duncan Schiedt saw him in Indianapolis, playing his first full-time job as a musician. He'd already had so much of life that he could sing blues about almost anything, and still be singing about himself — and he managed to give the feeling that he was always a little distant from it. It was his quick move back out of reach. He'd suddenly bang out some chords on the piano — start laughing as he was singing — do a little dance when he had to introduce his next number. He was giving his audience the truth, but not in a way that they'd be left uncomfortably holding it as he sat there at the piano in front of them.

It would be easy to say that it was Dupree's blackness that was the background for his blues — but that would be an oversimplification of Jack and his life. It's always difficult to be close enough to a performer to find what it is that makes him different, but with Jack you can see the things that happened to him — that toughened him. Just to say that a black man has the blues because he's black means that the response to the blues is limited to the skin, and things of the blues go on deep inside it. Jack usually gives July 4, 1910 as the date he was born, but he's said 1909 sometimes before, and the July 4th could be something that was just passed along with him. He was born in New Orleans, in the poor black New Orleans of old wooden houses that front on to the unpaved streets in the ramshackle neighborhoods of palm trees and scraggles of flowering vines. When he was two the first of the things happened that was to turn him into the guarded, self-directed man he is today. His parents were burned to death in a fire in their house, and he was left an orphan. He was placed in the same New Orleans Orphanage, the 'Colored Waifs Home For Boys', that Louis Armstrong, ten years older, had only recently left.

When he was released from the home he was just fourteen. New Orleans was an easy city — shabby and a little down at the heels — but it was loose and slow. You didn't have to have much money to scuffle along. But for Jack it was an empty, hard town, and he had to spend nights sleeping in abandoned automobiles until a woman with seven of her own children took him in. After that two men took over his education. One, a barrelhouse piano player named 'Drive 'Em Down', let him hang around him in the neighborhood bars where he played, slowly teaching him the piano style he has today. The other, a man named 'Kid' Green who ran a small gymnasium on Rampart Street, taught him how to fight. Before he was out of his teens he was boxing for money in small clubs. He still talks about his life in New Orleans, about what he remembers of the parades and the music. It was a town of music and slow, warm evenings, and little wooden barrooms on the corners where bands played for dancing on the weekends. 'Drive 'Em Down' was only one of the hundreds of pianists, but as the drummer Albert Giles said of a lot of the others:

'I never do hear "Salty Dog" played the way I heard it when I was coming up. Of course, some of the men was what you call specialists. "Salty Dog" was the only song they could play.'

In 1930 'Drive 'Em Down' died, and it was time to move on.

Moving on for someone like Jack meant moving north. California hadn't started to open up jobs to young blacks. Jack didn't have much besides his hands, but he went to Chicago to see if he could find something to do with them there. He scuffled, along with everybody else in the United States, through the Depression; a small, hard man, fighting or playing — whatever he could get to keep himself together. When he moved out of Chicago it was on a freight train, a few months before Duncan Schiedt saw him. The railroad police ran Jack and the other men on the train away from the railroad yards in Indianapolis, and Jack liked the looks of the town enough to stay around. Indianapolis is a flat, featureless town, with only a startling Civil War memorial to set it off from the other larger cities of Illinois and Indiana. It's east and south from Chicago, across the farm fields of midwest America. It had some blues. Leroy Carr had been living there when he died in the mid-thirties, and his guitarist, Scrapper Blackwell, was still playing around in some of the clubs.

Jack — without any kind of reputation — still couldn't have made it without fighting. A man named 'Kid' Edwards, who had a record shop on Indiana Avenue, got him some fights, and got some of the local club owners to listen to him as a musician. The Cotton Club was the first job.

Thirty years is a long time in anybody's life — and it's been a long time in the more than thirty years that have passed for Champion Jack since his days in Indianapolis in the early 1940's. He finally had enough going on with the piano so he could get out of the ring. His last fight was a ten round knockout of 'Battling Bozo' in Indianapolis in 1940, and his first recordings were made at a session in Chicago on June 13th, the same year. He went with a local bass player, Wilson Swain, and it could be Scrapper Blackwell playing the guitar on the first song they did, 'Gamblin' Man Blues'. Listening to the songs he did after all these years have passed there is the same immediate sense of identity that Jack has today. There is the same jabbing, staccato piano style — without much subtlety, hitting the piano like he was using his elbows. There is the same half-shouted vocal style, the voice simple and direct. And there's also some of the same direct honesty that has always been part of the blues. He insisted on the truth, even then, when it was harder for a black man to say what was on his mind.

My grandma left this morning,
with her basket in her hand,
She's goin' down to the warehouse
to see the warehouse man.
She got down to the warehouse,
them white folks say it ain't no use,
For the government ain't givin' away nothing
but that canned grapefruit juice.
It's a low, low down dirty shame . . .

There have been a lot of records for Jack since then, and they've all had this same rough directness. He was out of music for two years while he was in the U.S. Navy, then he came back to the piano and his blues. In 1959, after hundreds of small clubs and dozens of recordings, he got to Europe on a small tour. On a Saturday morning he got around to the Marquis of Grandby pub on Cambridge Circus in London, and he started drinking with some of the people from Doug Dobell's Record Shop, which was the most active outlet for his old recordings in Europe. One of the people drinking with him was Bill Colyer, who remembers Jack suddenly telling them that he'd be gone for a little while, but that they should keep his place at the bar. He was gone for half an hour, and when he came back he had on a new pair of shoes. They were the newest, new shoes in London — 'winklepickers' — two-toned, long and narrow. All the rest of the time they were drinking Jack kept looking down at his shoes. When he walked out they realized that he was going to stay around for awhile.

Jack's life since 1959 has been lived in Europe. Copenhagen for a time, Switzerland, finally England, where he's married now, raising a family, living away from London in a small village in Yorkshire. He's been free to sing as he wants, to live as he wants, and if the music hasn't changed that much it's because he was being honest those years ago when he was still spending half his nights in a sallow glare of ring lights, and the other nights in a bar playing the piano with hands still stiff from the fighting. He drives to most of the jobs in England, his name and occupation painted on the side of his car, and he usually gets there early so he can drink a little before he has to play. He never drinks much — just beer, sometime a little wine — mostly he laughs. He's seen so many young whites by this time that most of them look pretty much alike to him, and his moods of noisy laughter or sudden mistrust extend to all of them.

It's this sense of Jack Dupree that is the legacy of his blues — the strong core that gives his blues their identity. The hard beat, the sudden shifts of melody and harmony, the energy of what he does — then the darker moods of sentimentality or unhappiness. As a blues entertainer he's almost unique, and that's another side of the blues, along with the country intensities and the city shout, the blues as entertainment. With Jack in his pubs or his local concerts there's the same feeling that was described that night at his first club in Indianapolis. But with everything that's happened to him, with his new life in Europe, his years of success, there is still some of the uncertainties of his early life. He'll probably never shake off what happened to him in those early years.

At a job in the country outside of Birmingham Jack had to wait until almost midnight to go on, and then he realized that the people paying him were only students, and all they had to give him was a check. There have been too many bad checks in his life. He didn't want to leave, since he'd driven so far to get there, and there'd be no money if he didn't play. But he couldn't just go on stage without some kind of guarantee that he'd get some money from somebody. He stood up suddenly in the corner of the room and began talking to all of them. 'I know when you all see us coming to some place like this you think we got it made — but that isn't the way it is. We have to work for our money, and we have to keep going on out to where we can get our money.' It was late, he was tired, his short slight body was almost hidden behind the circle of sweaty shirts and upset faces. 'This is all we got, what we have in our hands here. Our talent is the only thing we got to get our money with, and it's no reason for us to give you our talent unless we get our money for it. You understand what I'm saying to you. It's all we have. The talent we have to do our music is all we have . . .'

Like the blues, he was saying something that had been said before — something he'd said before — but there, in the bare, dimly lit room it was still — in a final sense — the truth.

Sunnyland Slim

Sunnyland Slim

COMING TO THE CITY
- Sunnyland Slim

Well, I tell you the reason I left Memphis, a whole lot of people got peace of mind, they got to have it, and Memphis got a little rough and they closed the joints, and they was the places where they had pianos and you can be damn sure a piano player goin' to be closed with them. So I went to Missouri, around State Line, and I hung around there, but I had a reason to go to Chicago to be on a record. That's really the most reason I come there. I could make good money

133

down in the roadhouses, in all those clubs, but I
wanted to be on a record ... I don't say I like
Chicago, it's dirty and cold and it's got all that
politics, but I just come up to Chicago anyway.

Albert Luandrew stretching out his legs, looking out the
window at the gray April day. His musical name,
Sunnyland Slim, was given to him years ago — when he
was a lot thinner — but he still uses his full name when
he signs contracts or uses his passport. It wasn't only
Sunnyland moving into the cities — in 1942 and 1943,
when he got to Chicago, people were streaming off the
farms into the cities to get jobs after the long years of
the Depression. Part of the instability of American
society is this unending movement as people wearily try
to keep up with the prosperity they feel sure is
somewhere — if they can just catch up with it. There
was no provision for anybody once they got to the
cities — no city planning to take care of them — they
just moved in, and the musicians trailed after them.
Most of the people who got to Chicago in this period
seemed to be from Mississippi, and out of this loose
gathering of the Mississippi bluesmen came the Chicago
blues of the late '40's and '50's.

To someone like Sunnyland, who was part of all of it,
it still seems like it was as natural as sitting down to the
table to eat, even if it sounds like a kind of romantic
fiction. He was older than most of the others — 35 when
he got there — but they were all there together, and it
was the city, as much as anything else, that kept them
together. Like them Sunnyland had been born in
Mississippi; in Vance, about twenty-five miles south-east
of Clarksdale on State Route 3, on September 5, 1907.
But he'd been out of Mississippi for years, working
around Memphis as a piano player, then north around
the Missouri, southern Illinois country doing whatever
came along. Since he was older he'd had more experience getting by, and he met some of the musicians he'd
be working with later when he was still working his
hustles out in the country.

'Roosevelt Sykes was after me to come up there, but I was foolin' around. I had to get my fall house — I run a truck with the boys to do the cotton pickin' but that was over and I went back to the house I stayed at. In Carruthersville, Missouri, I was building dice for a white man there. He'd see a pair of dice and he'd get a picture of them and get me to build them and then he'd gamble with them. I was cuttin' hair, and pickin' cotton, and playin' the piano and I went into town and there was a harp player and a real black fellow sleepin' on the crap table, Little Walter and Black Honey. Walter was sleepin' with his head on the rack and Black Honey was on his guitar and the boss had to get him a pillow. I said to them I'm gonna go buy some groceries, and that goddamn rang a bell for Little Walter when I said I'd buy some groceries . . .'

The city was a new struggle for all of them, and it meant almost learning to live in new ways. It was something that everybody in the South Side, and the West Side, had to learn. They came up out of the South without enough education to do more than read and write, and a lot of the people hadn't even gotten that much. If they'd heard about jobs they still didn't know where to find them, and when they did find them they often weren't qualified enough to get them. It was mostly jobs they'd come to find — though it was sometimes just as important to get out of the South's racism. It wasn't that much easier in the northern ghettos, but there was some relief from it. The jobs were mostly poor paying and low skilled — sweeping up in a Gary steel mill or loading freight down at the docks — but there weren't any better jobs in Mississippi.

The urban bluesmen were an important force in this change — since they helped to bridge the distance between the southern life and the new city. Their legacy to the blues was the hard, unromantic look they gave to the city — and their refusal to be beaten by it. Whatever the black men and women of the South Side had to go

135

through during their work days — the scuffling hours of travel to get to the jobs, the crowds and the white hostility and the quasi-segregation of much of Chicago's area — when they got into one of the clubs at night they could get it all out with the blues. It was a language they knew, it was a sound they knew — and in the bluesmen they could see somebody who'd made it. To a hard-pressed laborer down for a drink from the tenement apartment he shared with three other families, the style and swagger of the bluesman was a visible sign that there was success there somewhere. The clubs themselves reflected it, with colored lights and tinsel decorations, and even to the cheapest jobs the musicians came in in slick jackets and processed hair, and music that was the latest in the blues.

The music had to be the blues. Sunnyland's first good job was at the Flame, and after he'd been there a week the club owner tried bringing in Lonnie Johnson, who'd been one of the biggest blues artists for nearly twenty years. Lonnie was so big that he'd almost gotten away from the blues, and Sunnyland remembers that Lonnie spent a week singing pop ballads like 'I Can't Give You Anything But Love, Baby' to nearly empty seats until Sunnyland came back in with the blues band.

The bluesmen themselves didn't do that well out of it. It was mostly $7 a night or $8 a night during the weekdays — for the men just up from Mississippi. They'd get more on weekends — sometimes $20 or $25 — but it was still a hustle. Most of them had somebody to stay with — a cousin or a sister, a girl they'd met at one of the clubs. The clubs were everywhere between roughly S. 30th Street and S. 50th. For someone with more of a reputation, like Big Bill or Tampa Red, there was a little more of an audience; they could get out of the city to play clubs in places like Indianapolis, but they hustled in the clubs along with everybody else. Tampa and Sunnyland worked for months together in a club in Gary, averaging around $20 a night even on weekdays. With a veteran club

136

musician's memory Sunnyland can remember how much he got paid at almost every club he worked in.

The big money could come in through the records — royalties on the sales and royalties on the compositions — and this is what they were there for. It was what had brought Sunnyland up, and he was like all the others. The new style of blues they brought with them was too confusing for the older companies to deal with, and for three or four years the situation was a hodge podge of semi-amateur operations and unstable companies — and great music. Sunnyland finally got the session he'd come to Chicago for in 1947, for the RCA blues line, which had only recently dropped its Bluebird appendage. The sessions were held at the old Victor studios in the big lakeside building north of the Loop. He'd worked a little with a blues singer named Peter Cleighton, who'd had some success in the early 1940's for Bluebird, under the name Doctor Clayton, so Sunnyland, who was completely unknown, recorded as 'Doctor Clayton's Buddy'.

Everybody was getting sessions for everybody else during this period, and it was Big Bill who got him the Victor date.

'Me and Big Bill needed some whiskey money and that man give me $700 — ooh, I never seen that kind of money — he give me $700 when I finished playing. Man, I was as happy as a sister in a C.C.C. camp.'

Bill played guitar, and Doctor Clayton's old pianist, Blind John Davis, played the piano. Sunnyland just sang. It wasn't the kind of blues that the younger musicians were doing — it was the kind of thing that RCA was phasing out of its catalog. The next year, for a small label called Aristocrat, run by Sammy Goldberg, Sunnyland put together the small session that, almost inadvertantly, marks the beginning of the new period of the Chicago blues. He was asked to get a session together with more than just himself and the bass player he was working with, Big Crawford. Goldberg asked him if he could get a guitar player.

'I knowed of Muddy Waters' people, but I didn't know Muddy until I come to Chicago in 1943. He was stayin' at 1851 W. 13th. I think he worked more in Mississippi than he was doing in Chicago, he was just workin' on that truck. But guitar players was scarce. Me and him met up on account of he come to the Flame and he come over to where me and Little Walter was, and he was playin' that bass style guitar and finally we got together for a job.

Sammy Goldberg said can you get a guitar player for the session and I thought about Muddy. I went and told them that his mother was dead and I got him off the truck. We was just hustlin' together — we'd cook us up eggs and greens — things to eat when we was on the job — and I got him to come down to Aristocrat.'

Muddy had recorded before, but at this time nothing had come out. He'd recorded for Alan Lomax in 1941 and 1942 when Lomax was collecting material for the Library of Congress, and he'd done a short session for Columbia in September, 1947. The Library of Congress material finally was released, but the Columbia sides still are unissued. The session he did with Sunnyland was his first released recording, and he went on from there, as Aristocrat became Chess Records, to become the dominant figure in the Chicago blues scene. They did four songs together, the first two, 'Johnson Machine Gun' and 'Fly Right, Little Girl', with Sunnyland singing. They were released with both names, *Sunnyland Slim and Muddy Water*. The next two were Muddy's, 'Gypsy Woman' and 'Little Anna Mae'. They did another Aristocrat session together as Sunnyland Slim and Muddy Water's Combo, then Sunnyland went his own way into the maze of small record companies that were springing up in Chicago.

If Sunnyland had just kept copies of the old 78's from this period that he sang or played on he could have a steady income selling them to collectors. Companies came and went. 'Companies switched up on me.' He recorded for Tempo Tone, Hytone, JOB, Sunny, Opera, Chance, Constellation, Cobra, and Blue Lake — along with occasional sides for the larger companies. Most of the time the musicians didn't get paid anything, if there were royalties they never saw them. Many of the masters were sold to other companies, but they never got a share of any advances paid to the small operators they'd recorded for. Sunnyland shrugs over it, 'I didn't care about nothin' but pussy, whiskey, and havin' a good time.' The worst aspect of it is that in most instances they lost their song copyrights — and with the copyright lost any future royalties that could have come in as the Chicago blues became known everywhere in the world. But Sunnyland was 40 when he started recording, and he had his own ways to get along. He's slowly getting back the copyrights he lost, and there's always the chance that some young group will do one of his old songs.

The same thing that happened in Chicago in the late '40's was happening in most cities of the United States. The people from Texas and Arkansas had gone west to Los Angeles and San Francisco — the Oakland, Richmond shipyards employed thousands of black workers during the war — and there were the same kind of small record companies there. Detroit, New York — there was the same press of people — the crowded, crumbling slums with new musical styles that responded to the experience of the ghetto. In New York it was bop — the musicians being exploited by dozens of small record companies — in Detroit it was another style of blues — centered around John Lee Hooker. But of all the urban blues styles it was Chicago's that finally dominated them all. Chicago musicians have so completely dominated the blues scene of the 1960's and 1970's — their music has reached such a wide audience — that there isn't much blues left in Chicago. Instead of in clubs on the South Side you have to look in clubs in Berkeley or Toronto or Boston — London or Copenhagen — to find Chicago's bluesmen.

All of this has come late to Sunnyland, but he takes it all with the same kind of cool appraisal he's given to the music scene for most of his career. Like the other Chicago men he's hardly there except to see friends. There was a large funeral for Muddy Waters' wife, who died in the early spring of 1973, and it was the first time many of the musicians had seen each other for months. Young men like Buddy Guy, who have let their hair grow, went unrecognized until they went over to give the word to Sunnyland and some of the others who'd been away. Buddy was in town to work in the club he's opened up, Sunnyland was back because the woman he'd been living with in Chicago wrote him that he'd been in California long enough. He thinks now of staying in San Francisco. 'There's no money to be had in Chicago.' Europe is alright — 'They treat you in the right way' — but he's in his sixties, and it's too far to go to start something new.

A musician like Sunnyland is conscious of the importance that the blues has had in the ghetto — he is conscious of the blues as a great legacy of poetry and music. And even as he's conscious of it he accepts it and goes on with the kind of club hustling he has to do to keep himself going. There is a sudden sadness when he sits down at the piano. He was stabbed in both arms in 1968 — his left shoulder opened up with a knife blade that went through the arm into his side. It was an ordinary South Side street robbery; they were after the ring he was wearing on his left hand. He starts to play and stops a minute to loosen up his fingers. 'It's half dead — everything I try to do with it.' But then the strength starts to come back — a little wine — usually sweet muscatel — a lemon and salt to suck on to get the voice open — and he's back to his blues again.

Sunnyland's music is a loose grouping of Chicago blues texts and melodies that he's given his own shape to. He's not like a Big Joe Williams, who just goes in to record and lets the songs come to him. Sunnyland works on his songs, and he writes them as he goes; in hotels and in his furnished rooms, practising them when he gets some place where there's a piano. He puts on his glasses, lights his pipe, and sits at the piano with his notebook. The words get written down, in a large careful handwriting, a verse at a time — three verses if it's going to be a slow blues — five or six if it's going to be fast and he'll need more words to make it long enough. The lines come to him in a phrase or a suggestion from something he's heard. He writes in pencil, usually getting the whole text onto the page, then he signs his name and address at the bottom — and keeps the song there until the next session.

The piano style Sunnyland's worked out over the years is the basic Chicago rhythm piano — but he started earlier, and he learned different things, and he uses them all. One measure will have a phrase from Walter Davis, for half a chorus he'll use a suggestion of Duke Ellington's left hand against pure Chicago fills in the right. It's something he's doing consciously. He sits and listens to a tape he's done and he talks about the different styles as they make themselves felt for a moment, then merge back into the whole context of the playing. It's only a glimpse — friendly and easy — letting his friends see a little of what he likes — to somebody who isn't into it it will only sound like brilliant, strong Chicago blues piano. The jobs he had to work all those years — 'It's five hours you know, so you got to mix in all kind of things' — left their mark.

The April day fades, the room is half in shadow, Sunnyland tries again to get the piece of paper loose that's blocking the bowl of his pipe. He starts to look through his suitcase for one of his publicity photographs. The telephone rings and he goes over to answer it. 'He says that there's something of mine on the radio.' Sunnyland puts down the phone and turns on a portable radio lying on the table. It's a Chicago recording — after half a chorus he smiles, 'That's Johnny Shines — me on piano, Dixon on bass.' He stands listening, half-smiling — then he goes back to his pipe. 'It's nice to hear those things you done before.' The recordings that he left the country to do all those years ago — when he and the Chicago blues were just starting out together.

Mighty Joe Young

Mighty Joe Young

YOU CAN STAY AROUND
Mighty Joe Young

For some of the younger musicians Chicago is still a world of small clubs and uncertain salaries and a neighborhood following. Even for bluesmen with a reputation outside the city there is still the problem of traveling. If you want to stay home with a family and children you have to take whatever jobs you can get. There isn't much money on Chicago's South Side — even less on the West Side, a ghetto even dirtier and poorer than the city's southern sections. Buddy Guy, who was very close to his young, growing family, gave up playing for awhile in the 1960's so he could spend his nights home with them. He tried working as an auto mechanic and it was steadier and the pay was better, but he couldn't stop playing his guitar. Mighty Joe Young stays in the bars and clubs scattered up and down Chicago's lake front, trying to stay close to home — but still worries that he might do better with his career if he could get out of town more. There is more money when you're on the road, but if you're paying hotel bills and eating in restaurants, buying gas and oil for the car, the money's going out almost as fast as it comes in.

You can get along in the clubs if you can play lots of different kinds of the new black music — 'the blues and then some' — if you stay then you do have the kind of special relationship that has been at the heart of the Chicago blues. To stay in the neighborhood jobs means staying with the black audience, and that sense of the interrelationship between the singer and his audience is unchanged — the bluesman as a symbol of identity for the people who have been pushed to the fierce physical limit that is the life in the ghetto — the bluesman as a symbol of the ghetto's tough, hard pride.

I always got the sense of this in the late fifties and the early sixties — seeing Muddy Waters play on the South Side, then seeing him away from Chicago performing for white audiences at a college concert or a folk festival. His regular club, when the band was in town, was Johnny Pepper's Lounge on S. 43rd Street, a low ceilinged room with the bandstand in the center, the bar almost meeting it from the back wall so the space was divided in two. The side nearest the door was left mostly clear for dancing, the other side had the tables and chairs. The band stand faced that way. It was a good club, and the people from the neighborhood in it were good people, but both of them were poor. The tables were worn, the decorations frayed, the floor rough and uneven, the carpet on the band stand was worn and threadbare. The people at the club usually had on their best clothes — suits, jackets, dresses for the women, stockings and high heels — but they had to work long hours at meaningless jobs that paid them almost nothing so they could come to Johnny Pepper's and dance on a Friday or Saturday night. For the whites who went the drinks were cheap, and most of the time there wasn't even an admission charge at the door; so they came in old clothes, or college clothes, and since they didn't dance they sat right in front, at the tables where you got the best of the band and the music.

Muddy is a man with an intent, still, personal dignity, and he brought that dignity to Pepper's. He didn't play for the first set — sometimes even for the second and third — waiting only for a last hour when it had gotten late and quiet. Instead he sat at a small table off to the side of the band stand talking a little to friends, signing autographs, smiling a little to the band — a large proud man whose presence dominated the room.

Then — a week later — a month later — I'd see Muddy again at a white concert — and the impression was often almost completely different. For a white club in New York he danced with the band, clapped his hands, smiled at the audience — for most of the set just entertaining. Only for moments would there be a flash of the other Muddy, when he would suddenly lift the guitar and sound a note with the slide on his finger, and in the moment of silence that always followed this his eyes would have their brooding dignity, and even in the white club there was the consciousness of his presence in it. In the sudden flash of pride it was possible to understand a little of how he could stay on the South Side, and what it was in his blues that helped make staying less of the bitter mouthful that had to be chewed every day, in every life, in Chicago's black slums.

Mighty Joe Young — younger than Muddy, but another bluesman from the same South Side — for him staying around has meant more than the commitment to be part of the other America. He has stayed close to his home, close to his family, changing whatever he had to change inside himself or his music to make it possible to stay. And in his gentle modesty Joe thinks of himself much more as a working musician than he does as a symbol of the insistent pride that keeps the ghetto alive. In an interview with Tam Fiori he said,

'I could be a jazz player if I really wanted to, but I figure that you have to be over average to sell as a jazz guitarist, and I don't figure I would be great enough to sell. So I wouldn't want to spend all my time fooling with jazz because basically I love the blues.

I gig all the time because of the way I play. The audience can come into any club where I'm working . . . and there are a lot of them who say: "We get sick of the blues," you dig. Well, I've got a message for them, because I can do more.

I do rock and roll also. I usually keep up with the top tunes and my band is clicking and they are ready, and this keeps me working . . . keeps me busy. I've always got a gig some place, no matter what kind of house it is.

If I go someplace where I've got to play blues all night, like a lot of these white kids like blues and at their concerts and things I can do that . . .and if I go somewhere I have to mix it up and play a lot of soul I can do that too. Basically I love the blues, but I love music, period.'

He isn't thinking of himself as anything more than a musician with a gig to play, but he has the same knowledge of what the blues represents.

'The blues is the feeling, and a true thing. And it is the hardships of black people. If I didn't go through all of it, my parents did.'

It's that knowledge of the blues that directs and shapes his music.

On a winter Saturday night in Waukegan I saw Joe do one of his jobs where they wanted him to mix it up, and he did have his message for them, too. As a club it was a lot like Taylor's Blue Lounge or the old Johnny Pepper's, but Waukegan's about forty miles up the lake, and on a frozen, moonless winter night the street was empty. In the white part of town the teenagers were doing their endless circling up and down the main street in their parents' cars — but in the black part of Waukegan there wasn't so much money for cars. And the club itself was away from the few lights there were — an old frame building called the 'Hawaii'. Inside the crowd was younger than it would have been at Pepper's, but there was the same strong declaration of what the music and the musicians themselves meant to the audience. The old blues were just old songs to the twenty year olds he was playing for — and there was some awkward confusion before they gave up trying to dance to them — but as he stood there with his guitar, going into the new blues and the new blues sounds, he did have his message for them.

The blues in the ghettos is a different music from the blues in the country South — but most of the musicians have the same roots. Joe grew up in Milwaukee — even further north along the lake — but he was born in Louisiana, and his first music was like Bukka White's, or even a little like Big Joe Williams'.

'I got involved in the music business from childhood. My father had an old guitar laying around the house . . . it was an old folk-type guitar.

I was really young, then, about seven, and I would wait until he went out, and I would get the guitar and try to play some of the things that I heard him do. I was pretty successful at this.

He didn't allow me to fool around with the guitar too much, because he figured I would bust it or something. So I would sit around and watch him play and listen to him. And I would keep the sound in my head and hum it, and when he'd go away then I would get the guitar and keep fingering it until I got that sound.

149

Eventually one day he went fishing, and I had the guitar and was sitting on the steps outside as I was the only one home, and I was playing it . . . we lived between two mountains, and I would run behind the house now and then to check if he was coming, and I'd go back and I'd play some more.

I played too long, and as I ran out to check, I ran into him and I'd left the guitar laying on the porch. From then on he bought me a guitar . . . and I had one and he had one.'

But the city blues isn't tied so closely to a countryside, or a country place. Wherever there's the ghetto there's the city blues. The big names, like Muddy, can tour from city to city and keep it up every night of the year. Joe heard his first blues band in Richmond, California — a shipyard town on the edge of San Francisco Bay just north of Berkeley. Thousands of black workers streamed out to Richmond for jobs during the war, and their music came with them. The band he heard was T. Bone Walker's, when T. Bone was at the height of his popularity. Walker was a Texas singer, but he was also one of the first real showmen with the electric guitar, and a lot of his stage appearance featured his guitar playing. For someone like Mighty Joe, this first glimpse of a blues guitar man was enough to turn him around. Lowell Fulsom came into town as well, and both of them helped to get him into music. The club scene in California didn't have the heavy closeness of the eastern cities, but the new looseness was beginning to open out the blues band sound.

After some lessons in Milwaukee, after he'd gone back to be with his mother, Joe was into the blues himself. He was in Shreveport, in Louisiana, for awhile in 1955; then finally came into Chicago. Every Chicago musician has to do a long apprenticeship, and they've all worked together in one club or another over the years. He was first with Howlin' Wolf, then Jimmy Rogers, Billy Boy Arnold, his own first band — then three years with Otis Rush. With someone like Otis he was the back-up guitarist — working the rhythm behind Otis' solos — but always the band works the first set without the featured artist, and Joe began the slow building that goes into getting your own neighborhood following. When he left Otis in 1963 he was able to get his own band started again. The next year he came in to play lead guitar on a Billy Boy Arnold album for Prestige Records, and he already had a local reputation. His leads were good, strong and capable, but they didn't have a real sting to them yet. It was an easy day in the studio — Billy Boy knew what he wanted on every song and he had musicians he knew with him — so Joe could lay back and fill in the spaces with a short, jabbing run, or open out the song with a variation on Billy Boy's line. Joe stood back against the wall, quiet and watchful, completely absorbed in what he was doing.

Waukegan is a dirty, drab town, and even in the winter darkness of the night I came up to see Joe's band the buildings of the main streets had a bleak feel to them, as if somebody had put them up without giving it much thought, using plans left over from a student's manual for brickwork. It was still difficult to reconcile the poverty of the black neighbourhood with the lavishness of Chicago's North Shore, even knowing that there were fewer jobs and a lower standard of living in Waukegan than there was in the South Side. The other America is a fierce and unrelenting place to live, and nobody in the small club was pleased to have someone like me in it. I was what kept the streets unswept, the houses in disrepair, the pay lower, the jobs fewer — and if it was something I wasn't personally responsible for, as a white I was a symbol of it. As much as anything else I was a raw irritant, rubbing an old wound, forcing the people in the club to see themselves from an outsider's eyes. A man in his early twenties was moving through the tables, his white shirt and the long handkerchief around his neck showing up in the darkness. I had some record album jackets with me so he could see what I was there for, but I was still there, and somehow a balance had to be established around me. He finally came and sat at the table across from me — not saying anything, but looking intently at me, the two of us sitting uncomfortably in the noise and the crowd around us.

Joe's band was working through all of it — nothing in anything they were doing showing that the club was out of the way and the crowd was small, and that there wasn't going to be much money for the job at the end of the long, sweaty night. They danced as they played, the sax players moving in elaborate loose patterns that went with the different rhythms the band was playing. Joe didn't try to force his music on anybody — the club was too small for any kind of elaborate showmanship — but there was a completeness to what he was doing. He had come out of this same background, and he was still in it playing his music. It's this kind of direct relationship between the bluesman and his audience that gives the city blues their kind of presence, their kind of immediacy. The music has to speak directly, and Joe did — in front of the small band stand — leaning over his guitar, the notes flashing with a full, heavy ripeness over the saxes and the drums and the bass.

A bluesman like Joe can move a little out of the boundaries that hem in the life in the city ghettos. If there isn't enough work out on road tours there's Europe, where an American black musician can keep working from country to country to a small, but determined audience. As we sat in the crowded office of the club, talking about what he wanted to do in the studio a few days later, sitting on narrow chairs against the partitioned walls while a pool game went on outside the door, he thought about Europe. For someone like Joe, Europe could mean some freedom to move around, to get out from under the worst weight of American racism — but he only thought of it as a place to try a new audience. 'I'd like to get a tour over to Europe, get a chance to play one of those concert things they have.' But would he want to stay in Europe — would he want

152

to get out of the other America? 'Europe'd just be a chance to get a little better known, you dig, and I wouldn't want to stay over too long, but I'd like me and the band to get over.'

So he stays — raising his family, living without any of the wild uncertainty that is usually associated with a bluesman's life, his music growing out of the speech, the sounds, and the life around him. The blues gives him a way to live in it, it gives him a voice — in the worn ghetto streets that have almost no voice at all.

Eddie Boyd and Memphis Slim

Eddie Boyd

Memphis Slim

YOU CAN LEAVE IT
- Eddie Boyd and Memphis Slim

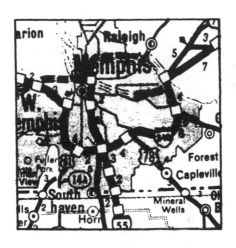

On a warm afternoon in the early spring of 1973, in Stockholm, Sweden, a group of musicians was doing some blues recording in a studio outside of town. The bass player, guitar player, and the tenor sax man were Swedish; the singer and piano player was a Chicago bluesman, Eddie Boyd, and the drummer was another black musician, Ed Thigpen, who'd recently moved from Los Angeles to Copenhagen. The session was going well; the young Swedes had been playing the blues so long they were as good as most of the session men you could pick up around Chicago for a casual recording date. Eddie hadn't been in a studio for two or three years, and he was feeling very loose and satisfied with the afternoon's work. There was a long break about 3 o'clock, and most of the musicians went out to get a sandwich, but Eddie and Ed Thigpen stayed behind. Ed wanted to know how he could find things to eat in Europe. Eddie laughed, he knew what Ed was talking about. 'That's true, man, they take a turnip, you dig, and they cut off the best part and throw it away. But I take the greens and I cook them up in my own apartment there.' Eddie, who's lived in Europe for many years, was telling Ed how he could find soul food. 'I have some land there, outside Helsinki — my girl's family owns it — and they let me grow my own. Just about everything you want to eat grows here — they just don't bother with it themselves.' It was a glimpse of one ex-patriot giving some advice to another, and it was also a casual glimpse of the life of an American bluesman in Europe.

Eddie Boyd is only one of the blues singers who's settled down in Europe. Memphis Slim and Willie Mabon live in Paris, and Champion Jack Dupree has his house and family in England. Why have they left the United States? The most important reason always is the lack of severe racial hostility in countries like France or Denmark or Sweden. These countries have their own prejudices and cruelties — but they don't extend to wandering black American musicians. The jazz artists began to leave the United States as early as the 'twenties, and the bluesmen were only following a well-worn trail. One of the first Harlem orchestras to go to France — Sam Wooding's — never came back, and some of jazz's most brilliant soloists — from Sidney Bechet to Don Cherry — have settled in Europe to escape America's racism.

And for the bluesman, also, there's work. Eddie can have much more of a career in Helsinki than he could in

Chicago. He went back to Chicago for what he thought would be a long visit in the summer of 1972, and he was back in Helsinki two and a half weeks later. Chicago's South Side was too violent, too dirty, too poor, and the rest of the city wasn't much better. The life in Europe still has its difficulties, but the bluesmen who've come have made their choice, and they intend to stay. Eddie would rather stay in Holland — 'That's my favorite country' — but his work permit expired and he had to move on. However, he shakes his head if someone suggests that he might go back to the United States if his work permit is questioned in Finland. 'I don't take any of the "Mr. Charley" or the Jim Crow stuff. If I had to leave Finland I'd move to one of those countries in Africa.' Sometimes, also, the job scene is a little difficult. As Memphis Slim described their situation,

'...you know, to be successful in the blues field you've got to play all type of blues, all styles, all beats. You can't stay in one rut, like quite a few friends of mine, very wonderful blues singers, but they were never known like they should have been, because when you heard one song you heard them all. But that's the way the guy felt and I think people should accept him like that. But it's not like that. You got to play a little boogie, a little song with a beat — and everything like that — to keep active.'

The bluesmen in Europe get along playing a little bit of everything in clubs or concert halls wherever they can get work. They'll go from two weeks as a solo performer in a little jazz club in Copenhagen, to a concert with some touring Chicago bluesmen in Switzerland, to three nights in a Swedish club with a rhythm section of amateur trad jazz musicians. Then it's back home for a few days — and then off again on another train or another plane, and the cycle starts again.

For Eddie Boyd his life has always been this demanding, and he's used to it, just as he's used to going his own way. It was his own sense of himself that forced him to leave the area where he'd grown up when he was still an adolescent. He was born outside of Clarksdale, Mississippi, on November 25, 1914, and his father was a bluesman himself, William Boyd. Eddie didn't see much of him, since he was always 'on location', but he did influence Eddie's decision to become a musician. It was his grandfather who raised him, and he managed to get in some schooling. He dropped out when the crops had to be planted, and then came back until it was time to do the harvesting. When he was about fourteen he had an argument with his step-grandmother and went to work across the river in Arkansas for a white man named George Crumble for a dollar and a quarter a day. It was while he was working for Crumble that he suddenly lashed out at the hard cruelty of the life that was facing him. He described what happened, talking with Mike Vernon years afterward.

'Out there we didn't have tractors or combiners, they had two horses and a hay-rake. So you go so far and you touch a trip-wire and would bail the hay and so forth, by hand. But that wouldn't clean the field real good so then they would get the boys, and I was one of the boys. When those guys would see old George Crumble and his horse coming, they was scared to say "here come the rider". Well I didn't take no notice, cause I was gonna work at a certain pace, cause I didn't want to work anyway! But I didn't never show no fear of him, and he didn't like that. You know what he told me? He says to me: "Say nigger, when the rest of the boys see me coming they move, how come you don't git no fear?" I said, "I'm working as fast as I intend to work, and if you don't like this man, you pay me off right now." Know what he told me? "I told you last year nigger, if you don't like de system round here, you better git away from here." I say, "I'm gonna tell you one thing fella: I was born here, and you came here as an agent on this plantation." The agent is a person who go round and sells things or creates something for a company. So he says, "I tell you, you's a bad influence." It took me two weeks to understand what he'd said! "I know what I'm gonna do; I'm gonna git off this horse and I'm gonna kick you a . . ." I said, "You try it, you . . ." And what I did froze every bone in his body, cause he raised his leg, and he got a forty-five on his hip: anyway, I hit him in the back with the hayfork, right in his crocker bone to paralyse him. And you know, between there and the state line of Arkansas was about a quarter of a mile and between the Mississippi River and where I was workin' — I had to move. When I left him with the hayfork hanging out the back of his back; he hasn't spoke today! And I walked — I never been able to swim — but see, God was with me! I went forward, and I said to myself, "Swim." And I kicked — and walked the waves. And I walked as far as I could — I guess I walked twenty minutes under water! And I came out in Tennessee: then I walked down the levee about sixty miles. Man, there was a thousand men come looking for me! Let me tell you something man. If you a Negro and you do something to a white man down there boy, there would be ninety-five thousand white people come to look for one man — and I was only a little boy . . . So that's how I left my home town.'

He stayed in North Memphis, and further out of town in a little place called Woodstock for the next few years. First he played a kazoo with a little country dance band, then he learned the guitar, and finally he learned enough on the piano to play 'every song on the market' — all in the same key, B flat, 'and I hates that key now.' Out of town where he was living there were a lot of little country juke joints; rough barrooms with a piano and some scarred tables and chairs, the inside usually so dark you couldn't see much except the dim outline of the bar running along one of the walls. For awhile he was in a cafe close to the gates of the Fisher Plant; then with a small band in the juke joints. When he thought he was ready he moved on — and he went into town to work on Beale Street. It was still a hustling scene, and there were a lot of piano players around, but he got a job in one of the bars. He was working either with a band called the 'Dixie Rhythm Boys', with Eddie Childs on trumpet, and Alex Atkins — who later played with J.B. Lenoire — on clarinet, or playing the blues by himself. He was the steady bluesman at a place called Pee Wee's for awhile — getting paid a salary of $7 a week for seven nights work, from 8 p.m. to 8 a.m. the next morning. But he insists, 'That was glamorous to me man!' By the time he was in his mid-twenties he'd worked in clubs and juke joints over most of western Tennessee, across the river in Arkansas, and north to the Missouri line. It was time for him to move on again.

'I went to Chicago. Went by Greyhound bus. My uncle was living in Chicago maybe ten years before I went there, and I lived with him. He was on the West Side: I lived with him for about three months and then I moved over the South Side with Memphis Slim, as he had a club there. I had already worked with Sonny Boy Williamson. See, Memphis Slim, Sonny Boy, Big Bill and some drummer, whose name I forget, they was all together. Sonny Boy was a harmonica player and the Union didn't consider him to be a musician, so he wasn't in the Union. But I joined the Union as soon as I got there. So I played behind Sonny Boy. And at that time he was playing at the Triangle Inn on 14th and Blue Island. He was very popular, this was in '41.'

It was the usual scuffling life of the South Side musician. Noisy, smoky clubs, long hours on the band stand, sleeping late when there wasn't any day job, hanging around with the other musicians whenever there was a night off. It was a rough, but thorough preparation for the uncertainties of the life he was to lead in Europe thirty years later. He managed to stay out of the Army by working days in a meat packing plant that was preparing food for shipment to Russia. What he was doing was essential; so he was deferred. It wasn't until 1947 that he was able to record — as 'Little Eddie Boyd'

162

with J.T. Brown's Boogie Band for Victor Records. It was the same kind of slow apprenticeship that a lot of other bluesmen were putting in at the same time. There were some more sessions for Victor — nothing very big — then for four years there was only one single with Regal records. He's never been a man to be turned aside when he wants something, and he decided that the problem was with the way he was being recorded. He felt he had to go ahead on his own.

'. . . I knew I'd got it but I wasn't getting the right breaks. So I was working saving me some money little by little. I started working the steel mill for eighty-eight cents an hour. But I didn't work for that figure very long. I guess maybe four weeks. I was getting enough money to cut my own session, so that way I could cut it like I wanted to. If I fail then I would have no one to blame but myself. So that's what I did, and I guess in about six months time, starting off at eighty-eight cents an hour, I kept getting promoted, I guess I must have been making about sixty dollars a week to take home, that would save me twenty dollars a week for the recording session. . .'

The song he recorded was 'Five Long Years', and he leased the master to J.O.B. records in Chicago. In three weeks it was the biggest selling R & B release in the United States, and the song is still one of the popular standards with the South Side bluesmen. Eddie got a Chess contract out of it, and started the series of one-night stands that goes with being a 'name' artist. Like so many others he pushed it too hard on a long night drive. He was using St. Louis Jimmy as a road manager, and Jimmy smashed the band's station wagon on a stretch of highway south of Milwaukee. Only the two of them were in it, but both men were seriously injured, and the station wagon was completely destroyed. '. . . After a while he picked up speed, and he went dead straight into a huge elm tree. That tree was 120 years old, the tree didn't even budge, the car just wrapped around it.' Eddie was in a cast for more than three months, and almost all of his money went into medical bills and expenses.

Even more than the loss of money, and the injuries he suffered, was the loss of momentum to his career. He hadn't been able to follow 'Five Long Years' with anything as successful, and after the months off the road he was almost back at the place he'd been ten years before. The accident was in 1957, when he was 42, and it was a long, discouraging struggle to get back again. He bought a farm sixty miles out of Chicago and raised chickens and grew vegetables, working it in the summers when he didn't have so much work in the South Side clubs. He was ready for a change, and when he had a chance to go to Europe with a blues tour in 1965 he took it. In Europe his life began again, and he sees no reason that he should give it up.

Part of the legacy of the blues that we've been given by the singers living in Europe is their insistence that we can't forget America's racism. It's something they would have had to keep silent about when they were younger musicians, but all of them were angry and resentful at what they'd had to face. Eddie Boyd always sings 'Black, Brown, and White' when he's doing a club date, and part of Champion Jack Dupree's concerts is always a long spoken blues where he talks about what he had to go through. This same insistence, this same anger, is also part of the music of the singer who's probably the best known of the ex-patriot bluesmen, Memphis Slim. Meeting him, you don't have a sense of this anger. He's a tall, imposing man, with only a gray streak in his hair to show he's almost sixty, and despite all the confusion that goes on backstage at a concert he's able to sit quietly through it all, almost at a distance from it. It's only when he talks, when he plays and sings that he describes how he feels, how he responded to the racism that faced him everywhere.

One of the reasons for his quiet calm, is that he began as a musician very early, with the support of his family, and he's had a long successful career. He was playing in Memphis about the same time as Eddie Boyd, but their lives were very different. Memphis Slim's background was almost middle class, while Eddie was getting along as best he could on the north end of town. The two men began playing at about the same time, and Memphis Slim is only a year younger. He was born as Peter Chatman in Memphis on September 3, 1915, and his father — also named Peter Chatman — encouraged him from the beginning. His father played both guitar and piano himself, although he never played professionally. By the time Slim was 16 he was working in some of the same small clubs Eddie was to work in a few years later. He also heard a lot of the other pianists working in the city — among them Speckled Red, Theodore Cox, and Roosevelt Sykes. In Chicago, later, he and Big Bill Broonzy became close friends and they had a lot of things they agreed on, as well as a lot of things they argued about — and one thing they were agreed on was that when he first came to town his playing sounded just like Roosevelt Sykes.

'You could say I adopted the Roosevelt Sykes technique on the piano. He was my influence in the development of my piano style.' Slim's comment on it. Bill remembered — in his book *Big Bill Blues* — that he told him, 'You sound just like Roosevelt Sykes ... He got mad at me, but then he found out what I meant. He changed and went to playing like Memphis Slim.'

Slim had set out to be a success as a musician, and as soon as he felt sure enough of himself he got out of Memphis. One of the most widely distributed blues record labels in the late 'thirties was the Bluebird series coming from Chicago, and most of the best known bluesmen in the country were Chicago based during this period — so it was Chicago he went to. 'Transplanted', is the word he used for it, and usually remembers that it was 1937 when he got there. He was twenty-two, and he'd already had five or six years of blues playing. The first of what were to be hundreds of recordings was done in 1940, in August. Lester Melrose, who was working with nearly every blues artist in Chicago, got him the date for Okeh, the other important blues series. There was a small band that included Washboard Sam, and they did six titles. They were released under his own name, Peter Chatman.

For someone like Slim, who was completely professional in what he was doing, and could sing almost any kind of blues, there was a steady demand from the blues companies. Only three months later he was back in the studio again, this time for Bluebird. These came out as Memphis Slim, possibly because there were already the Peter Chatman sides on the other label — and also he was skinny, came from Memphis, and a lot of the musicians were using nicknames. The first side he did for Bluebird — 'Beer-Drinking Woman', on Bluebird B-8584, he remembers was a hit, and he was on his way.

The blues record industry was still struggling to build back up its national distribution after the dreary years of the Depression, but already there were singers who had almost a national reputation. One of the most successful was Big Bill Broonzy — and for someone as ambitious as Slim, Big Bill was an important man to be associated with. Slim joined Big Bill's band in 1940. As he remembers,

'Chicago is the first place where I met the late Bill Broonzy. When his piano player Joshua Altheimer died in the late 1939 I was the only piano player there that seemed to satisfy Big Bill at that particular time, 'cause Big Bill had a particular way of singin' the blues . . . so in 1940 I started playing piano along with Big Bill on Chicago's West Side. Big Bill Broonzy and the late Sonny Boy Williamson and myself were working at Ruby's tavern. That's where all the guys used to come from the South Side late at night when they'd got off from work. Tampa Red, Big Maceo, Jazz Gillum, Roosevelt Sykes, the one and only Curtis Jones, the boy that made that number "It's Lonesome In My Bedroom" . . .'

166

He still jokes about the job at the club — 'When I was playing at Ruby's I was paid weekly — very weakly.' But he went on from the job with Bill to his own career as a major blues artist. Bill said that he was responsible for Slim's decision to go out on his own. He remembers saying, 'You're good enough now to go on your own. You don't need Big Bill or no other blues singer with you. Just get you some good musicians to play with you and you'll be Memphis Slim, just like I'm Big Bill.'

Memphis Slim not only went on, after the war he had much more of a career than Big Bill did. The blues had changed to either a heavier, more electric sound — the Chicago sound of Muddy Waters — or a more sophisticated small combo sound — like the bands Roy Milton or Bobby Bland had formed. In 1946 and 1947 Memphis Slim began recording with a band that was first called 'Memphis Slim and his Solid Band', then in 1947 for Miracle Records, 'Memphis Slim and his House Rockers'. He had two sax players — Alex Atkins on alto, and Ernest Cotton on tenor. In the first couple of years there was no drummer — but there was a series of bass players, among them Ernest Crawford, Willie Dixon, and Charlie Jenkins.

The sound of the House Rockers wasn't more than blues-tinged, but it was tight, clean, professional, and his singing and piano playing kept it all moving. This was the usual sound of all of Slim's bands — solid musicianship, but with the drive coming from Slim's fingers, like the motor down inside a slick looking car, that for all its slickness would just sit there without the motor under the hood. After ten years of the House Rockers in 1958 he was recording as 'Memphis Slim and his Orchestra', on still another label, Vee Jay Records, but the blues was changing again, and the city sound that Slim was identified with was changing with it. He had to shift again, and only a year later he'd found the direction to move. He followed his old friend Big Bill into the folk blues.

The blues has always had a duality to it. One of its sides is its personal creativity — the consciousness of a creative individual using it as a form of expression. The other side is the blues as entertainment. Someone like Memphis Slim is a professional blues entertainer. But the blues is a style of music that emphasises integrity — so how does a singer change his style without losing his credibility as a blues artist? It's not an easy thing to do, and many bluesmen have never been able to solve the problem. Slim seems to have been able to do it because of the strong personality he shows in both his recordings and in his appearances.

For Slim, as well, there was another side of his music that he was able to emphasise. He'd always been a good pianist, and in his years of traveling he'd heard a lot of piano music. He seems to remember a little boogie or instrumental blues from every town he ever played in. As early as 1951 Big Bill had started recording in Europe with his own guitar as accompaniment, and in 1956, through Pete Seeger, he started recording for Folkways Records, the leading folk music label in the United States. Sensing what was happening Slim began to shift over to the new audience. In the summer of 1959 he recorded for Folkways, with only his own piano as accompaniment.

Slim has always been able to get sessions together, and when he has the feel of the kind of music that's getting a response he has no difficulty moving into it. Over the next eighteen months he was almost a one-man recording industry. There was the New York Folkways session on July 19; and a month later, on August 18, he recorded thirteen songs for Vee Jay in Chicago with his old orchestra. Before the end of the year there were two more Folkways albums, one with Willie Dixon on bass. In January, 1960, he and Dixon did another album for Verve; then in April he, Dixon, and Pete Seeger did two more albums for Folkways. Three months later he was in Europe, and he recorded in London on July 14, and Copenhagen on August 25 and 26. Two months later he was recording again in New York for Folkways, and then over the fall there were four lps for Prestige. He started the next year, 1961, with two albums on January 16 for Candid records.

After so many years working as part of a band it was remarkable that Memphis Slim could begin again as a piano soloist — but he is a good pianist, with an unmistakable feel for the rhythms and the melody patterns that was part of a wandering pianist's every night repertoire. His right hand has a kind of nervous excitement as it runs through flowery strings of notes and clusters of chords — but the left hand has an open, steady rhythm to it — calm and assured. It's almost as if he were saying, go ahead and get worked up, there's always something steady here to come back to.

His voice is just as good as his piano playing. It's strong, and he can use it for uptempo shouts or the slowest half-spoken blues. Of all the things that are effective about his singing the most important probably is the sense he gives of a personal sincerity — even if it's a song that doesn't seem to have any kind of meaning to him. He seems to be saying that he's there behind any thing he says, right there steady through any kind of trouble. When he was still a singles artist on the old black radio disc jockey programs the sincerity was one of the things that helped sell his records.

It isn't only in Memphis Slim's music that you get any of the sense of why he felt he had to leave the United States. In his own personality you understand the sense of personal dignity that took him away from the pervasive insult of a segregated society. He's come through all of it with an intense dignity — almost a careful aloofness in his relationship with the world around him. He refuses to accept the difficulties of black life in the United States, and he thinks of himself as an artist who has a role in the society he lives in. If it has to be Paris where he can get the kind of respect he's earned with his music — then Paris it will be, and he's no longer prepared to make any compromises in his life about it.

It's this sense of personal integrity that is part of what Memphis Slim has given to the blues, and part of it, as well, is his total professionalism. Few bluesmen have been able to continue such successful careers over such a long period. It is also the busy, striding optimism of his playing and singing, and the combination of all of these things has given him his place in the blues world.

He seems conscious of it himself, as he sits listening to an interviewer's questions, smiling gently as someone backstage comes up to talk to him. He bends down to hear what they're saying, still the tall, easy figure of some of his old photographs. He's usually wearing a jacket — sometimes a suit — looking more like a businessman than a bluesman. The stage hands come through with some wiring — loudspeakers — he steps carefully out of the way, still looking down at the person talking with him. He's unworried, unhurried — sure of where he's come to and sure of how he got there. The people running the concert come to find him, he excuses himself from the people he's been standing with, talks a moment with the man who will introduce him. The lights come up, the applause starts — then fades away into the darkness of the hall. Memphis Slim crosses the stage, smiles, sits at the piano — and in a moment he's playing — singing — with all the concentration of a man who'd been thinking just about this performance for hours before. Somewhere in that first moment is what Memphis Slim is as a bluesman and as a human being — a professional, who is proud of his profession — a blues singer who is proud of the blues he sings.

Lightnin' Hopkins

Lightnin' Hopkins

'I WAS BORN WITH THE BLUES'
- Lightnin' Hopkins

The sun hangs low over Houston's sprawling black neighborhoods — the streets drying from an afternoon shower, the trees and bushes shaking off the water in the faint stirring of the wind. On a quiet back street Lightnin' Hopkins has gone outside to sit in front of his apartment, drink beer from a can wrapped in a paper bag, and talk desultorily with friends. 'You want a beer?' he asks. 'I can have somebody run over and get it for you.' He sits on a low, gray painted railing, wearing

173

his dark sunglasses and white cowboy hat, watching the people pass by. Jokes and laughter with the women who go teasing past — shouted questions to the men who slow down in their cars to wave. There's a small grocery store across the street from him — small and old and shabby, with ads for chicken pieces and green beans hand painted in wavering letters on the windows. Just behind the grocery the old houses have been pulled down and there's a twisting concrete ramp of a freeway overpass. It's after five o'clock and the traffic is jammed up as far as the eye can see, inching along in a spew of gas fumes, soiled heat, and rumpled tempers. Lightnin' sits and watches it go by, then he shrugs. 'It take a lot out of a man to sit caught like that every day. Never could do it myself.'

Lightnin's apartment — on the ground floor of the new building behind him — is modern, furnished with the newest appliances, and parked right in front of it are two new Buick sedans, one for himself and one for his wife. Lightnin's done well for himself, and he can watch the commuters sweat by with a certain philosophic detachment, smiling to himself behind the dark shadow of the glasses, gesturing with the rumpled paper bag around his beer can. It's almost become a cliché to describe the poverty and the alienation of the country bluesmen, and here is Lightnin', in his sixties now, living in relative comfort in a neighborhood he's known all his life, with the wife he's been with since 1944. 'Now I'm getting old I just want to sit quiet, do what playing I can that's not hard to get to. 'Course, they always been after me. I could play every night if I wanted to — and if I didn't have to go up in no airplanes.' A car pulls over to the curb and a man rolls down the window, leaning out to say something to Lightnin' in a low voice. They talk over some private business, Lightnin' nods, the window is rolled up, the car starts up again. A horn is sounding feebly over the glistening backs of the cars behind the store, the afternoon clouds over again, and a few drops of rain come slowly along the street, brushing against

174

the bushes as they pass.

His life now seems so natural to him that it's difficult to remember that he had to face the same harsh struggle as most of the other bluesmen, and he had to wait a long time before his blues brought him anything. He was born in Centerville, Texas, a small farm community north of Houston on March 15, 1921; so he grew up through the collapse of the farm economy in the late 1920's and the desperate years of the Depression that followed it. He was eighteen in 1930. He still feels that it was the vicious poverty of his early years that gave his blues their reality.

'Now you know the reason that we had the blues? The reason we had the blues was because we had something to have the blues for. We had to get up in the morning, we go to bed at 8 o'clock to be sure and we get up in the morning, man, it's six. We wash our face and eat our breakfast, we grabbed a mule, man, and put a bridle on him. We go to the field and we plow that row. Well, what can you have but the blues? All you can do is sing down that row behind that mule. You got the blues. Alright, that'll give you time to think about it, that you got something before you. But here's what you would think. You will be hoping that what's in your heart, that someday that you will not have to be walkin' behind a plow. You understand? And when you get to hoping that, you get a hold of something. That's when you really got the blues, you got the blues, baby. Alright. Well, I hate to tell it all about what I did, but I was plowing a mule one morning and I knowed that I had the blues. I tied the mule to the post and walked on across the field. I kept going across the field. I kept on goin' . . .'

It's later in the evening; he's sitting in his living room across from a T.V. set with the sound turned low. There's still a little of the early years left on him. His body is still thin and hard, his hands still have scars from the plow lines and the farm machines he struggled with when he was a boy. But he thinks about it, laughs a little. "Course I guess they got their mule back.' He stayed in the country, working a small farm north of Centerville, but he was already involved in music and the blues. The blues was so much part of his childhood and adolescence that he still remembers the old singers the way most people remember baseball players or football heroes. Bessie Smith, Blind Lemon Jefferson, Texas Alexander. The names come up again and again. He's told the story of his first meeting with Blind Lemon many times — about the Sunday afternoon picnic of the General Association of Baptist Churches at Buffalo, Texas, when his father drove the family up on the back of a flat bed truck, over the narrow dirt road that wound through the rolling farm country. He goes back to it so often — not only because it was his first meeting with Blind Lemon — but because it's almost the place where his life as a singer began.

'This is true. When I was in Centerville, Texas, just seventeen miles from Buffalo, Texas, I was eight years old when I went with my guitar. It was near 'bout as big as me. That big. I went to the Buffalo Association and met this here big blind man, Blind Lemon Jefferson. That man was pickin' that guitar and I just felt it was in me. I told them, I say, "I can play what that man's playin'." They knowed I could play, all of them young boys there; so I got up there with my little old guitar and I hit it. Blind Lemon looked, he — you know — turned around. He got the sound from me. He say, "Who is it?" and they say "This here boy can play a guitar." And he called at me, "Boy, you got to play it right," and I was scared a little bit, you know, but when I said something he heard I was just little and he say, "Let me hear you play that guitar a little bit, boy." I hit his note, runnin' through there like he was, you know. He say, "Boy, what your name?" I told him, "Sam Hopkins." He say, "You know, I believe you can play," and he hit his guitar and I was in tune, 'cause I tuned it out there. Man, he put me up on top of that truck where he was sitting and we had a association! I played on top of that truck and he told me, said, "Boy, I didn't think you could play like that." Told me to keep working, and I been at it ever since . . .'

But he was different from most of the young singers growing up at the same time. He was close to his family — to his mother and his brother Joel and his sisters — and he wasn't much of a traveler. So he stayed in Centerville, got married, and worked for six or seven years for an older man named Lucien Hopkins that he thought of as his 'uncle'. He was still playing, but it was something he kept for weekends, for little country dances in the shacks back of Centerville. He knew about Houston, and he knew a little about the chances for performing there, but he was too close to his life in the country to leave it behind. Also he was close to his cousin, Texas Alexander, one of the best singers from Texas to record in the 1920's. Texas didn't play, and he always needed an accompanist. It was with Texas that Lightnin' had his first experience on a Houston stage — but it was the older man who was nervous about performing.

'I tell you, my cousin Texas Alexander, out of Leone County, I came to the Rainbow Theatre here with him and that man had been singin' for three or four years, had records out and different things, you know. Man, right there, and I was a little old boy — about fourteen years old when we came down here to the Rainbow Theatre, and you know what he done? He got stage fright! He had to walk off. He started a song, and I knowed the song he was goin' to sing and I just continued playing. And they were pattin' for me. Man, they just give it to me and Texas he had to go back, you know the boys that had him up there went back with him, but when he come back, boy, he sure did sing.'

It was Lucien Hopkins who finally got him to try singing for a living. About 1946 — when Lightnin' was thirty-four — Lucien told him it was time he should start, and helped him buy a new guitar. Lightnin' and his wife moved into south Houston, and he worked for awhile with Texas Alexander, who was still doing some singing in the local clubs. But the record business was beginning to revive after the effects of the war and the shellac shortages and the recording ban, and small companies were springing up in every city. Lightnin' was soon approached for some recording by the local talent scout for Aladdin Records, a new company in Los Angeles. The woman who was signing the artists wasn't comfortable with Texas Alexander, who had spent some years in prison, but she took Lightnin', Amos Milburn, a pianist from Houston who was twelve years younger than Lightnin', and a pianist who was working with Lightnin', Thunder Smith. It was from Thunder that he got his recording name; since one of the duo was called 'Thunder' the record company thought it was natural to call him 'Lightning', and the name stayed with him, although the 'g' was dropped along the way. Many of the details of his activities of these years of his life are still a little vague, but he was back in Houston a few weeks later, and the recordings for Aladdin weren't particularly successful when they came out. But the next year he became involved with a young veteran who'd started a small company in Houston. The man was Bill Quinn, and the recordings Lightnin' did for his Gold Star label started him on his career as one of the most important country blues artists of the post-war period.

The story is that someone working for Gold Star heard Lightnin' sitting on a curbstone playing his guitar for some children and told him to see Quinn. Most of what Gold Star had been recording was local country music, but there was considerably more interest in the blues, and Quinn moved into the field. Lightnin' recorded with his brother Joel playing second guitar, and Quinn hurried out a release of 'Short Haired Woman' and 'Big Mama Jump' on Gold Star 3131. He remembers that it sold between forty and fifty thousand records, without any real advertising and with only local distribution. Lightnin' was clearly a sensation. He went on recording for Gold Star until the company went out of business in 1951, and each record sold about forty thousand copies, and some of the bigger hits like 'Baby, Please Don't Go' sold as many as eighty thousand. But the money slipped through Lightnin's fingers, and to keep up with his style of living he recorded for other companies at the same time, and Gold Star had to compete with records by other companies that were better distributed. It was a point of friction between them that Quinn still brought up when he first talked about Lightnin' twelve years later. Aladdin was in Houston in February, 1948, and Lightnin' did some more recording for them — and there were small sessions with other companies. But his best early recordings were the Gold Star releases, and they have become scarce collectors' items.

At this time the radio was the most important way for a blues artist to reach his audience, and *The Country Blues* described the effect of Lightnin's early recordings.

'When radio stations played Lightnin's records on Gold Star, there would usually be an awkward silence after the record was finished while the announcer tried to think of something to say. Usually there would be a nervous laugh and he'd say something like, "That Lightnin', he sure is something isn't he?" Lightnin' was a little bewildering to most people who heard him. He was accompanying himself on an unamplified guitar. There was no piano, no drums, no bass. He was one of the first blues singers to work without a group in ten years. His singing was very free, almost disorganized. Some verses were twelve measures long, some were thirteen and a half, some were ten. Lightnin' sang in the same unmeasured, harsh style that Lemon Jefferson and Texas Alexander had recorded twenty years before. The guitar trailed along, echoing the words, droning in a rhythmic drumming on a lower string then ringing above the voice between the lines and carrying off painfully intense, lyric passages between the verses. Even the blues themselves, rough and direct, were a far cry from the recordings of other blues singers. Lightnin' was one of the roughest singers to come out of the South in years, and his singing seemed almost primitive when his records were played on afternoon record programs, between endless commercials and the singing of popular stylists like Billy Eckstein and Nat Cole.'

But it was the rougher, more intense young singers like Lightnin' who were getting heard through radios in places like Chicago and Detroit and Los Angeles and who were to change the mood and direction of the blues. It was the period when Muddy Waters was recording for a small company in Chicago, when John Lee Hooker was making his first records for a company in Detroit. They had a hardness, a directness, that older men like Tampa Red or Big Bill couldn't match. They were still, however, local artists, and the companies putting out the records had to struggle for distribution, along with all the other difficulties of production and manufacturing. Within a few years all but a few of them had sold out to another company or gone out of business. Quinn was doing well with Lightnin', but he couldn't keep up a series of hits with other artists, and he couldn't sell Lightnin's releases outside the Houston area. In 1951 he sold thirty-two unreleased masters Lightnin' had done for him to Modern Records and went out of business. For the next six years Lightnin' recorded for blues labels in New York and Los Angeles, sometimes signing exclusive contracts, sometimes not bothering. He was still going through money, but there seemed to be an endless stream of it — just as there seemed to be an endless stream of blues.

One of Lightnin's unique gifts as a blues artist is his ability to improvise a blues about almost anything. He uses four or five basic melodies and guitar accompaniments and he builds a particular type of blues with each of the different approaches. He also has a good memory for other blues, and he can work with the melody or theme from something by Blind Lemon or Smokey Hogg and turn it into something distinctively his own, while still leaving an elusive suggestion of the original in the final version. One of his other gifts is his phenomenal guitar technique. He has a loose, shrugging style that gives his shuffles a feeling of complete ease, while his fingers are flashing on the strings. And he alternates the faster pieces with the long, suspended running passages of his blues pieces. Once, driving him around Houston to pick up a guitar, we had to get an instrument with a broken string – and it was pushed onto the back seat until we could get to a music store for some strings. It was a gray, gusty morning, neither of us thinking about much, but the car had to stop for a red light beside a school and some little girls were walking along the sidewalk on their way home. Almost without thinking about it Lightnin' picked up the guitar and began playing and singing a blues about the girls. It wasn't possible to tell – without watching his fingers – that the guitar only had five strings – or that the blues was only something that was coming into his mind as he sang it.

Combining his gifts, and working with a drum and bass player to make his sound a little more modern, Lightnin' did 190 blues during the years he was recording for the commercial blues market. Some of the companies were small, like Jax and Sittin' In With, but he also recorded for larger companies like Mercury and Decca. With his usual facility to create a blues about anything happening around him he recorded a blues called 'Sad News from Korea' for Mercury in 1951; then finished the story with 'The War Is Over' for Decca in 1954. There were recordings on TNT, Harlem, and Ace labels – thirty sides for Herald Records. But by the mid-1950's he was losing his commercial touch; his records were selling fewer and fewer copies, and his style was losing out to the Chicago band blues.

By 1959 Lightnin' had all but dropped out of sight. The only lead to him was a cousin who was working as a cook in a place in New Orleans where a lot of musicians ate. In Houston everybody knew him, but nobody knew where he was. He and his wife had separated, and the address the local pawn broker had was an old one. 'Sam's guitar's in and out of here all the time,' he said, but he didn't know where he was living. Neighbors knew where a sister was living, and the sister answered a door in an old, peeling wooden building. From *The Country Blues*:

'You lookin' for my brother?'

'Yes.'

'He's moved over to Hadley Street. Look for the house with the red chair on the porch. Somewhere down from the corner.'

At the house on Hadley Street, a nervous, heavy woman looked out from the darkness of her small living room. A television set was flickering in the corner. Had she seen Lightnin'?

'This time of day he's usually at that barroom at the corner; if he's not there try the one across the street. He'll be at one or the other.'

He wasn't at either one. The next morning a green sedan rolled alongside the car at a traffic light on Dowling Street. A thin, nervous man leaned out the window.

'You lookin' for me?'

'You Lightnin'?'

'That's right.'

As the cars drove slowly along the street he agreed to record that afternoon.

The recordings we did that day — with a rented guitar and a portable Ampex tape recorder in Lightnin's shabby room — became the famous Folkways lp that introduced him to the modern intellectual audience for the blues. It's this audience, with its festivals and university concert series and its lp record racks, that has given him

182

the new apartment, the two Buicks, and his unconcerned smile as he watches the commuters struggling
along the overpass in front of him.

But there is a shadow in the background of all this,
even for Lightnin' as he opens another beer and turns to
say hello to a woman going into the grocery store. There
seems to be no way for the blues to go on when there
are no men like Lightnin' left. The blues is a legacy —
something that's being handed on — but there doesn't
seem to be anyone to hand it on to. Lightnin' talks
about it as he drinks his beer. 'Some of the white boys
got a lot of it. You know, they can play their guitars
and they can even sing pretty good now. But it
isn't — you know — goin' on through with it.' Something's gone — something in the language, something in
the way of life. It could even be the lines of cars
squatting on their concrete tightrope. It could be that
they've taken something away that can't ever be
brought back. The direct connection between the
moment — and the blues that's the response to the
moment has blurred, dulled. Lightnin' thinks about it
again, tries to say what he's thinking, finally puts the
can down on the ground to hold up his hands.
'I see a few young musicians coming along. I do. But
it's not many. It's not many at all, and the few that
is — I'll tell you, you know what I mean, they don't
have it. They just don't feel it. I don't know why
they don't feel it but it just isn't in the young ones I
hear, and they all come to me.'
He looks away, smiles, shakes his head.
'I never had that trouble. I had the one thing you
need to be a blues singer. I was born with the blues.'

AN APPENDIX

This book has grown out of a series of recordings suggested by Dag Haeggqvist of Sonet Records. The intention of the series was to record, or to gather, blues by as many as possible of the last great blues artists. At the same time the series has tried to show the blues in all of its styles and forms, from the early Mississippi blues of Big Joe Williams and J.D. Short to the modern Chicago band style of Mighty Joe Young, and from the raw country sound of Lightnin' Hopkins to the urban sophistication of Memphis Slim. The series is under the general supervision of Samuel Charters, but other producers and researchers who have contributed material used in it include Chris Strachwitz, Ed Denson, John Fahey, Quint Davis, and Clyde Otis.

A NOTE ON SOURCES

Most of the artists discussed in the book were interviewed by the author, including Big Joe Williams and J.D. Short, Bukka White, Robert Pete Williams, Champion Jack Dupree, Sunnyland Slim, Mighty Joe Young, Eddie Boyd, Memphis Slim, and Lightnin' Hopkins. In addition interview material was used from a number of other sources. Mike Vernon's interview with Eddie Boyd was published in his *R & B Monthly*, No. 24, January/February 1966. Tam Fiori's interview with

Mighty Joe Young was published in *Melody Maker*, October 7, 1972, and Max Jones' interview with Snooks Eaglin was published in the same weekly on January 16, 1973. Charles Edward Smith's description of Big Joe Williams is from his notes to the Folkways Records album *Big Joe Williams and his Nine-String Guitar*, and Duncan Schiedt's sketch of Jack Dupree is from his notes to the OKeh album *Champion Jack Dupree/ Cabbage Greens*. Dr. Harry Oster's interview with Robert Pete Williams is from the Folk Lyric album which he produced, *Angola Prison Blues*.

Both Tom Mboya and Robert Blauner are quoted from *Americans From Africa*, edited by Peter I. Rose and published by Atherton Press, Inc., New York, 1970. The quotes are from Volume 2; Mr. Mboya from page 412 and Mr. Blauner from pages 417 and 440. William A. Stewart's article 'Understanding Black Language' was published in *Black Americans*, edited by John F. Szwer and published by Voice of American Forum Lectures, 1970. His article appeared on pages 131-143. *The Country Blues*, quoted in the text, is by Samuel Charters and was published by Rinehart in New York in 1959. *The Bluesmen* is also by Mr. Charters and was published by Oak, New York, 1967. The Son House material is taken from *The Bluesmen*, but was originally published as an interview with Julius Lester in *Sing Out* magazine. Bill Quinn, discussed in the chapter on Lightnin' Hopkins, was originally interviewed for *The Country Blues*. Albert Jiles, in the chapter on Champion Jack Dupree, is quoted from Mr. Charters' book, *Jazz: New Orleans*.

The spiritual quotations in Chapter 6 were compiled from a number of magazine articles published in the late Nineteenth Century, and the quote from the black song leader is from the article 'The Survival of African Music in America', written by Jeanette Robinson Murphy and published in 1899 in the *Popular Science Monthly*.

DISCOGRAPHY

GNPS-X 10010

THE LEGACY OF THE BLUES SAMPLER

BUKKA WHITE, Aberdeen Mississippi Blues, SNOOKS EAGLIN, Funky Malaguena, CHAMPION JACK DUPREE, Found My Baby Gone, MIGHTY JOE YOUNG, Wishy Washy Woman, JUKE BOY BONNER, I'm A Bluesman, BIG JOE WILLIAMS, Black Gal You're Sure Looking Warm, MEMPHIS SLIM, A Long Time Gone, J.D. SHORT, Starry Crown Blues, ROBERT PETE WILLIAMS, I'm Going To Have Myself a Ball, EDDIE BOYD, The Cannonball, SUNNYLAND SLIM, She's So Mellow, LIGHTNIN' HOPKINS, Please Help Poor Me.

GNPS 10011

VOLUME ONE
BUKKA WHITE

Aberdeen Mississippi Blues, Baby Please Don't Go, New Orleans Streamline, Parchman Farm Blues, Poor Boy Long Ways From Home, Remembrance of Charlie Patton, Shake 'Em On Down, I Am In The Heavenly Way, The Atlanta Special, Drunk Man Blues, Army Blues.

Recorded in Memphis, Tennessee, 1963

GNPS 10012

VOLUME TWO
SNOOKS EAGLIN

Boogie Children, Who's Loving You Tonight, Lucille, Drive It Home, Good News, Funky Malaguena, Pine Top's Boogie Woogie, That Same Old Train, I Get The Blues When It Rains, Young Boy Blues, Tomorrow Night, Little Girl Of Mine.

Recorded in New Orleans, June, 1971

189

GNPS 10013

VOLUME THREE
CHAMPION JACK DUPREE

Vietnam Blues, Drunk Again, Found My Baby Gone, Anything You Want, Will It Be, You're The One, Down And Out, Roamin' Special, The Life I Lead, Jit-A-Bug Jump

With Huey Flint, drums; Benny Gallagher, bass; Peter Curtley, guitar; and Paul Rowan, harmonica. Recorded in London, 1972

GNPS 10014

VOLUME FOUR
MIGHTY JOE YOUNG

Rock Me Baby, Baby Please, Just A Minute, Drivin' Wheel, Wishy Washy Woman, Early In The Morning, Sweet Kisses, Lookin' For You, It's All Right, I Have The Same Old Blues.

With Bob Reidy, piano; Sylvester Boines, bass; Alvino Bennett, drums; Charles Beecham, trumpet; Walter Hambrick, tenor. Recorded in Chicago, 1972

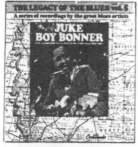

GNPS 10015

VOLUME FIVE
JUKE BOY BONNER

I'm A Bluesman, Problems All Around, Trying To Get Ahead, If You Don't Want To Get Mistreated, Lonesome Ride Back Home, Funny Money, I'm Lonely Too, Real Good Woman, Come To Me, Yammin' The Blues, Better Place To Go, Tired Of The Greyhound Bus.

Recorded in Berkeley, 1972

GNPS 10016

VOLUME SIX
BIG JOE WILLIAMS

I Been Wrong But I'll Be Right, Black Gal You're Sure Looking Warm, When I First Left Home, Little Annie Mae, Levee Break Blues, Hang It Up On The Wall, Lone Wolf, This Heavy Stuff Of Mine, Tell My Mother, Big Fat Mama, Back On My Feet, Jefferson And Franklin Blues.

Recorded in Stockholm, 1972

VOLUME SEVEN
MEMPHIS SLIM

Everyday I Have the Blues, I Am The Blues, A Long Time Gone, Ballin' The Jack, Let's Get With It, Only Fools Have Fun, Broadway Boogie, Gambler's Blues, Freedom, Sassy Mae.

With Eddie Chamblee, tenor sax; Billy Butler, guitar; Lloyd Trotman, bass; Herb Lavelle, drums. Recorded in New York, 1967

GNPS 10018

VOLUME EIGHT
J.D. SHORT

Starry Crown Blues, My Rare Dog, By The Spoonful, You're Tempting Me, Slidin' Delta, I'm Just Wastin' My Time, The Red River Run, Help Me Some, East St. Louis, Make Me Down A Pallet

Recorded in St. Louis, 1962

GNPS 10019

VOLUME NINE
ROBERT PETE WILLIAMS

Woman You Ain't No Good, Come Here, Sit Down On My Knee, Angola Penitentiary Blues, Late Night Boogie, Goin' Out Have Myself A Ball, Poor Girl Out On The Mountain; Graveyard Blues, You're My All Day Steady And My Midnight Dream, Keep Your Bad Dog Off Me.

Recorded in Baton Rouge, 1972

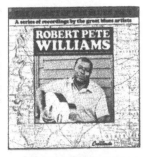

GNPS 10020

VOLUME TEN
EDDIE BOYD

Lovesick Soul, I'm A Fool, Kindness For Weakness, Tell The Truth, The Cannonball, Black Brown And White, It's A Mellow Day, Do Yourself A Favor, Dedication To My Baby, Zip Code.

With Peps Persson, guitar and harmonica; Christer Ecklund, tenor; Rolf Alm, bass; and Ed Thigpen, drums. Recorded in Stockholm, 1973

VOLUME ELEVEN
SUNNYLAND SLIM

Couldn't Find A Mule, Gonna Be My Baby, Woman
I Ain't Gonna Drink No More Whiskey, Days Of
Old, She Got A Thing Goin' On, She's So Mellow,
Get Hip To Yourself, Bessie Mae, I Had It Hard,
She Used To Love Me.

Recorded in Stockholm, 1973

VOLUME TWELVE
LIGHTNIN' HOPKINS

Please Help Poor Me, Way Out In Abilene, Don't
You Call That Boogie, Swing In The Backyard,
The Hearse Is Backed Up To The Door, That Meat's
A Little Too High, Let Them Little Things Be True,
I Been Burning Bad Gasoline, Don't You Mess
With My Woman, Water Fallin' Boogie.

With Ira James, harmonica; Carl 'Rusty' Myers and
Ozell Roberts, bass; and Larry 'Bones' McCall,
drums. Recorded In Houston, 1974

19985277R00113

Made in the USA
San Bernardino, CA
21 March 2015